MARTIN BUBER AND CHRISTIANITY

HANS URS VON BALTHASAR

Martin Buber
& Christianity

A DIALOGUE BETWEEN ISRAEL
AND THE CHURCH

Translated by
ALEXANDER DRU

THE MACMILLAN COMPANY

NEW YORK

NIHIL OBSTAT:
HUBERTUS RICHARDS, S.T.L., L.S.S.
Censor deputatus

IMPRIMATUR:
E. MORROGH BERNARD, VIC. GEN.
WESTMONASTERII, DIE 8 APRILIS 1960

The NIHIL OBSTAT *and* IMPRIMATUR
*are a declaration that a book or pamph-
let is considered to be free from doctrinal
or moral error. It is not implied that
those who have granted the* NIHIL
OBSTAT *and* IMPRIMATUR *agree with
the contents, opinions or statements
expressed.*

*Originally published in German
under the title of*
EINSAME ZWIESPRACHE

PRINTED IN GREAT BRITAIN
© HANS URS VON BALTHASAR 1958
© IN THE ENGLISH TRANSLATION HARVILL PRESS 1961
ENGLISH TRANSLATION FIRST PUBLISHED IN THE
UNITED STATES OF AMERICA BY THE MACMILLAN COMPANY

Contents

Preface

For anyone to embark upon a discussion of this kind will seem to most people a complete waste of time, a pointless and fruitless anachronism, fated not to arouse the smallest interest. For it can be said without the least hesitation that no subject is so carefully skirted, no point so deserted, as the point at which the one chosen people of God is related to itself as Old to New Covenant—that centre point in the world's history which supplied Hegel with the idea of the dialectic of history. It is true, of course, that the discussion is carried on tirelessly in books which purport to explain the twofold Covenant, and that it has given rise to literary and theological problems of endless diversity. But the heirs to those two traditions, the individual men who represent them, have lived apart for two thousand years without ever coming face to face or trying to see what sort of a person the other might be. Yet their situation, their very existence one may say, involves them in a conversation which it is not in their power to terminate, one which leads immediately into problems which extend beyond the sphere in which individual and people are entirely free and engages the whole of our being. If it is to be a real conversation, and a fruitful one, its range must therefore be such as to reckon with heaven and earth, and so it will always hark back to the conversation held on the Mountain of the Transfiguration, when the Son of Man conversed with Moses and Elijah: συνλαλοῦντες One

7

of the witnesses to that scene was Peter (2 Pet. 1, 16); and as he listened the prophetic word acquired for him its ultimate certitude—'and they spoke of his decease that he should accomplish in Jerusalem' (Lk. 9, 31). Whatever the two peoples say to one another will always have to preserve an echo of that conversation.

In *Two Forms of Faith* Martin Buber ventured on to that deserted field and carried his lonely dialogue up to the point at which, in his opinion at least, the only intelligible attitude was silence. His final conclusion was that the two forms of faith are irreconcilable. That judgment is acceptable in the world, but it is not one that invokes the grace of God. His discussion of the subject is profound, dignified and severe, which is what a discussion of this kind should be. Leaving aside the preliminary compliments and conventional gestures that have once again become usual, he goes straight to the matter. In the course of replying to him, we shall not feel tied to that particular book, but will take the whole work of Martin Buber, who is now over eighty years old, into consideration, making it the subject and occasion of the pages that follow.

CHAPTER ONE

Author and Work

MARTIN BUBER is one of the creative minds of our age. Most of those who know something of the riches of his work, and have felt the appeal of his personality, are alive to one of the aspects of a many-sided man: the sage, the philosopher of religion, the anthropologist, the originator of the 'dialogical principle', and the brilliant translator of the Scriptures who achieved what Herder and Hamann and the romantics always longed for, a translation of the Hebrew in which the genius of the semitic language sounds through the German without distorting it. Furthermore there is the man who saved the Hassidic tradition, and worked tirelessly to restore and interpret it. And finally there is the theoretician and 'theologian' of present-day Judaism. Those who know him at all realise that he is not simply another writer of Jewish race who has been admitted to the German Pantheon, but the man, and, what is more, the only one, who remained in the forefront of German literature throughout the last half century, representing the Jewish race in the face of a blind hatred of everything Jewish.

From the days of Moses Mendelssohn and his grand-children in the Biedermeier salons of Berlin, down to the period of Hermann Cohen and the philosophers of the turn of the century, the tendency among the Jewish intelligentsia has all along been one of assimilation; their aim has been to present the spirit of Jewry as broadly humanistic. Martin Buber's work flies in the face of that long literary tradition, and his whole endeavour has been to recapture the essential spirit of Judaism, and to recollect its nature. He has expounded his reflections in a classical German untainted by those fatal lapses of taste which mar the work of some Jewish writers, and its form no less than its content disarmed the equally fatal prejudices against the Jews. That wholesale reversal of a centuries-old tradition deserves to be pondered.

There were others besides Buber who pursued the same end with a similar energy and power: Franz Rosenzweig and Leo Baeck among others, and, on a different plane, Chagall. But although they sought to present an unweakened, undistorted picture of Judaism in a language intelligible and palatable to the contemporary western mind, it is precisely in those circles that Buber's originality stands out so clearly. It is then that one can appreciate his architectonic and strategic sense, his capacity for combining delicate feeling for what is just and right with an innate sense for what is proper and fitting at the time,—his grasp of the specific weight of ideas, their relations and their situations and the constellations they form and of the system of co-ordinates in which to insert the structure of thought created by his own genius. His is a carefully reckoned, if ultimately very simple, monumental structure, solid on all sides; and it is not easy to find a weak spot in it unless it be, perhaps, the point on which our theme is focused.

Buber not only has an eye for the individual spiritual figure but for the context in which he has to be seen. He also possesses that strong sense of the factual and real which is characteristic of his race. 'The important thing,' he writes, 'is to realise how tremendously difficult it is—and then to believe, to believe nevertheless. Such was my feeling from youth up. An unblinking, fearless vision—as unlike optimism as is pessimism.' (1) 'I am no visionary,' he writes elsewhere, 'though I think I have vision.' (2) And again, 'I have no "teaching." I only have a function: to draw attention to certain realities.' (3)

The motto which St Thomas Aquinas chose to designate the character of his work was *sapientis est ordinare:* the wise man's task is to bring about order. The same thing can be said in a sense of Buber's work, for the questions which he asks are these: How much of the Jewish tradition is still valid, and what has ceased to matter? Where can we find a solid foundation? What do the origins and sources of Judaism mean to us today—Moses, the Law, the Kingdom, the Prophets, the Apocalyptic element? What have the Rabbinical tradition, the Kabbala, Spinoza and Mendelssohn to contribute? Is there any significance in the Hassidim? And how exactly do Marx and Freud stand to the foregoing? What about Zionism? Of what real importance are the thinkers and poets who have most influenced our age?

The answers which Buber gives are all of them marked by a sure sense of direction, and nothing is left to chance: there is barely room even for the play of life itself, for the movement of change and becoming; anything new that claims admission must present itself in the form of a development.

There is no trace anywhere of experimentation, and his one concern is to verify reality here and now. However varied the foil-play of his argument, Buber invariably ends by bringing everything back to the Jewish situation in history. His Lectures on Judaism, which in various forms are the theme which has been the accompaniment to his long life, provide a sort of basic study of the Jewish fact in the world, whether present-day Israel as a people or as a country care to recognise it as such or not.

Buber's claim is to have freed the idea of Judaism of its historical ballast, and of everything extraneous and unimportant, so that as a result of that clarification and simplification it can be recreated in terms valid in the present. His aim has been to make Judaism understandable and its demand peremptory. That is why the Christian really has no choice; he cannot refuse him a hearing whether he finds the work sympathetic or not. The subject itself obliges him to reply.

Since the foundation of the Church, a dialogue between Jew and Christian has always been rare and invariably brief. Judaism shut itself off from Christianity, and the Church turned its back on the people which rejected it. The history of their relations and contacts is, it must be confessed, dispiriting. The penances, persecutions and sufferings imposed upon the Jews in Christendom were usually looked upon simply as a just expression of God's punishment, and not, which would have been more Christian, as an addition to the mystery of suffering which the Church contemplates in the Cross: they point and lead on to the bottomless misunderstandings and the endless theological short-circuits that followed. In that atmosphere the dazzling eschatological light that falls on Israel from the 11th Chapter of the Epistle to the Romans, which had hardly been mirrored in the works of Origen (4) before it was once again obscured, is not so much as noticed. Nor was it that light which penetrated the ghettos and opened the door to discussion in the age of enlightenment and liberal Protestantism. It was not in fact very difficult to reach agreement on the basis that Jesus was a religiously and prophetically gifted individual who respected the religion of his fathers which he purified and spiritualised (5)—though where was the gain? Those concerned were content to discuss irrelevant and trivial differences in terms of the philosophy of religion. They were really at one before they began. But where, in the last two or three centuries, is there any hint of a genuine dialogue?

Argument and agreement are worth nothing unless they get down to the difficulties, and can only be carried on in virile terms. Provided power and superiority are not in the balance, and as long as the subject itself is honestly served, and the individual conscious of his religious duty, hard-hitting does not interrupt the lines of communication or disturb the dialogue. It must be admitted, however, that there are times when it looks as though an ultimatum had been delivered, as though the point had been reached when a final breach was unavoidable. This is illustrated in the manner in which the two leading exponents of the 'dialogue' now writing—Buber and Jaspers—talk about the Catholic Church. What they say can only imply an accusation against the Church of a total incapacity to enter into a dialogue consequent upon its ineradicable dogmatic impatience. Among the Christians with whom Buber admits to having achieved a genuine relationship he does not mention one who is not anti-dogmatic, not to say liberal. (6). Not one Catholic is named. On the other hand, it must be added that while quite a lot has been written on Buber's work from the liberal point of view, particularly on his religious philosophy, the harvest on the Catholic side is very meagre (7); though one must honestly say that Buber never refused to enter into discussion with anyone who genuinely offered to do so (8).

In the last resort, of course, it is the subject that counts and not the individual who represents it. He can only express and explain it, giving it form and perhaps style. But the subject always looms up, mysterious and many-sided, behind him, far greater than its representatives. And as for the Catholic Christian who speaks for the Church, what can he know of the greatness he has to represent so inadequately? It would be a sad state of affairs indeed if he only reckoned with the external, human aspect, and confined himself to defending that side only. Yet what does he know of the mystery of the People and of the Kingdom of God, the fullness of Christ and mankind saved? What can he know of 'the holy tree' and the branches that are cut off and those that are engrafted? How shall he interpret the mysterious words of the Lord in the Gospel where he says that Israel will not see him again until . . . or the Sermon of St Peter that seems to offer Israel every hope? How many questions there are in the background, behind the Christian, and to which there are no ready answers! But in the full confidence that on both sides there is always much beyond what is said we are justified in making a start even though humanly speaking there does not seem to be much hope. For St. Paul was always taking up his task in the Synagogue anew not from some private whim, but out of obedience, so we can rest assured that the task itself is genuine enough, and, what is more, one that will never be over and done with.

CHAPTER TWO

The Source and the Living Voice

CHRISTIAN AND JEW have lived together for two thousand years, but one may well ask whether Christians since the days of St Paul have ever felt conscious of being addressed in a way that touched them directly as Christians. Indeed one might justifiably ask whether relations between the two peoples ever advanced beyond the point at which the Christian felt called upon to enlighten his blind and stubborn brethren and help them on the right path; whether they ever advanced to the point of becoming an intellectual and spiritual relationship and what Buber calls a dialogue; so that the Christian might expect to receive something vital and alive from the Jew, something more than the letter of the Scriptures as they were handed down, something that could not be divorced from the living voice, very necessary perhaps, and bearing upon salvation.

The Christian attitude, generally speaking, can be summed up approximately as follows: the Jews forfeited their mission when they failed to recognise Christ as their Messiah; they had, in consequence, to hand over the books which belonged to them up to that time to be administered by those who had become the people of God. They forfeited the prerogatives which had belonged to them as the chosen people and those prerogatives devolved upon the King-Messiah. The fulfilment was given to the Christians, and with it all the promises: the Old Testament now belongs to them alone, since they alone can read it as it is meant to be read, as a witness to Christ; eternal life is with him, and it is an error, a mere 'opinion' to look for eternal life without him in the scriptures (Jn. 5, 39). The refusal with which the Jews met the fulfilment of the promise determines the Christian picture of the Old Covenant retrospectively and splits it into two unequal parts. On the one hand, there are the 'stiff necked,' who declared their refusal from the first, and who 'could not hear' the voice of Christ, whose father is not Abraham but the devil (Jn. 8, 44). Of them Augustine says, with reference to the end of Matt. 23: 'Why should the blood (of the prophets) be upon them who lived long before they were born, if not because they form one race, one dough, one lump of impiety to which they cohere by imitating one another? For they did not bear the word of God within them; they only had it in the books they read.' (1) On the other hand, there are the messengers of God and the elect who believed beforehand in Christ, pointed towards him, died for him and are hidden members of the Church to come. Their words and their works now manifestly belong to Christianity, whereas the function of the others is at the most to testify, by their continued existence among the nations, to all they have lost. 'The Jewish people was deprived of its dominion and dispersed all over the world, in order that it might be compelled to bear witness to the faith whose enemies it had become. Having lost the Temple, the Sacrifice, the Priesthood, and even the Kingdom, the Jews can only preserve their name and identity as a people around the remnants of the old sacraments . . . in the same way that Cain was marked so that no one should kill the man who had killed his brother out of pride and envy, and because he was a just man.' (2) How was it possible for a single word to reach the Christian and make his faith vibrate in response, if it came from men who had already been expelled from the Covenant of God by the prophets, and were 'sunk in a deep and heavy sleep'? (3) 'Those who fell away from the faith of Abraham, forfeited Abraham's legacy. The Jews degenerated and were lost; we became the followers of Abraham, and won.' (4) So little is to be expected from the Jews that it is a waste of time to listen to what they say—for if it is not of Christ that they speak, they speak in vain.

It would be worth examining the precise form of the breach in communication between Christian and Jew which has lasted for two thousand years.

For some time past now Christians have begun to doubt whether, in allowing that situation to develop, they had been entirely loyal to all the facts of their New Testament faith. What St Paul implies in the last chapter of the Epistle to the Romans, with all its theological and historical implications, is a very different thing. At the beginning of the Epistle he shows that the Jews, as bearers of the promise, had a great advantage over the Gentiles (3, 1-2), and yet derived 'no advantage' from it (3, 9) because Abraham, by reason of his faith in the grace of God's promise, became a just man, and so 'the father of us all' (4, 1). He was appointed the bodily father of the Jewish people, the bearer of the promise (though empowered by faith alone, since, like his wife Sarah, he had become sterile [4.19]) *and* appointed the father of 'many nations', Israel's neighbours, related to them by blood and in communication with them: the image (as can be seen in the perspective of the fulfilment) indicates a deeper and fuller communication in the prefigurative and fruitful faith of Abraham, the real spiritual father of all those who are really

Have been loyal to Scripture?

inducted into the living form of his faith: 'who against hope believed in hope', 'not weak in faith' but 'strengthened in faith, giving glory to God, most fully knowing that, whatsoever he (God) has promised, he is able also to perform' (4, 19-21).

As the concept of fatherhood indicates, and as chapter 11 then demonstrates more precisely, the fact that the Gentiles are implanted in Abraham's faith implies more than a mere convergence and meeting in a common prototype: it means being 'engrafted' into the 'olive tree', spliced into its 'root' and 'participating in its sap' (11, 16-17). 'For if the first-fruit be holy, so is the lump also: and, if the root be holy, so are the branches.' The two parallel images in 11, 16, may possibly suggest that since the first image clearly refers to the Israel of St Paul, to the holy remnant that has been converted to Christ (11, 15), the same interpretation should be given to both images. But this is impossible, because the whole agglomeration of Israel, the real, physical people, organised in tribes, proclaims its descent from Abraham. The two images apply both to the holy, historical 'root', the faith of Abraham, of the Patriarchs, Kings and Prophets, as well as to the spiritual 'root', that 'remnant' to which St Paul and the other apostles belong, that belongs inwardly to the justifying faith of Abraham, which is faith in the promise. If that were not so, the fourth chapter would lose both point and force. The spiritual children are grafted into the root that they may share in the living sap of the holy olive tree, but not in such a manner as to by-pass the bodily Israel since 'God hath not cast away his people, which he foreknew' (11, 2), and because 'the gifts and the calling of God are without repentance', (11, 29) but so as to become part of that indivisible and living whole which grows naturally (*kata physin*, 11, 24) starting from the Patriarchal root and leading into the Israel of the New Testament.

The Gentile Christians are admonished to be humble, for by comparison with that natural development they have been engrafted 'against nature' (*para physin*). Nor does that admonishment imply that the two categories are of equal standing once they have been spiritualised by the New Covenant; on the contrary, there is a clear suggestion of one-sided dependence: 'thou bearest not the root; but the root thee' (11, 18). And the objection that 'the branches were broken off that I might be grafted in' (11, 19) is doubly rejected. The dialectic of 'rejection' and 'reconciliation' (11, 15) is, as it were, a purely Old Testament matter (11, 2-10); the Gentiles are included in the all-embracing event only on condition that once taken into the holy tree, they behave as believers in the sense of Abraham, which would of course be ruled out by any sense of pride or superiority. In this context St Paul does not go beyond the point of view expressed in the theology of the Exile which certainly interpreted the dispersion of Israel among the Gentiles, the 'breaking off' of the branches (11, 19), as a punishment, but also saw it as an event relevant to the salvation of all nations in and through Israel, whose mission was to bring home the converted, bearing them upon its shoulders. (Is. 14, 22; Bar. 5, 6).

In the light of St Paul's teaching one is therefore prompted to ask whether the Christian who belongs *para physin*, against nature, to the holy tree, might not, at some moment in his life of faith, undergo a very particular experience touching the origins and source of faith: the experience of being inwardly moved by the sap that rises from the holy root on which he is engrafted, which he must to some extent regard as different, foreign or perhaps primitive, and only 'his own' as a result of that indescribable experience. The experience is indescribable because there is no point in the world from which to compare the Old and the New Covenant. The usual form in which Christians grasped the relationship, resulted historically, in stressing all that they recognised as their own and assimilated; whereas the other factor, the opposing element, the dissimilarity, is almost entirely overlooked. The condition of the *one* people of God was changed: it was transformed through Christ, and from having been concealed in the image and hidden in the prototype, it was made manifest, intelligible and revealed. *Novum in vetere latet.* The new is latent in the old: one can unseal the Old Covenant, break it open, take out the kernel and throw away the husk. The obverse is not quite so clear: *Vetus patet in novo*, the old endures in the new—not so clear because, from a Christian point of view, with the coming of the new there is no longer any old, except in the recollection of the words of the Scriptures, and the sight of those 'whose senses were made dull' and who are the very opposite of manifest and open: 'For, until this present day, the self-same veil in the reading of the old testament remaineth not taken away, (because in Christ it is made void') (2 Cor. 3, 13-14).

But for decades past, biblical research has made it increasingly clear that historical truth, in Jewish history no less than elsewhere, can never be reached by the use of the simple recipe of the husk and the kernel. And although the fruit of that scholarship no doubt calls for the revision of a somewhat hasty notion of Revelation, it is at the same time so apposite, so 'natural', so impressively enriching and broadening, that we accept it almost unconsciously, grateful for the increase in our knowledge that has transformed a hitherto two-dimensional picture, giving it the depth and relief of a third dimension. Biblical Revelation is not an unmediated word falling from heaven, addressed to a more or less recalcitrant people through the instrumentality of individual men, either orally or in writing; it would be truer to say that revelation originally becomes 'incarnate' in historical situations, and that the experience of them only ripens gradually in the course of time as it is assimilated, pondered, and handed down. We are now able to discern in the texts the Jew's much more profound, more existential participation in the very substance of the word of revelation, so much so in fact that the word of revelation simply cannot be separated out from *cf. Levie* the articulate human response, like kernel from husk. Although the word of God never coincides with human history, nevertheless it reveals its sovereignty—its judgment and its grace—in the depths of that history. It is never an abstract word addressed to man, but the articulation of the convenanted union between God and man. The word of God requires the unweakened accompaniment of man's answer in prayer—the cry of David, Jeremias and Job, and the words of comfort that the deutero-Isaiah addresses to his suffering brethren. Although the personal note of the individual often sounds through unmistakably, it is not the individuals, but the voice of the nameless crowd of those who prayed and suffered in Israel, who carved the words of God out of their hearts, words which remain the words of God to the Christian, and are still the daily prayer of the Church in the recital of the Psalms.

The final consequence of all this is that we now see more and more clearly how deeply rooted primitive Christianity is in the Jewish *milieu*. In the heyday of the liberal interpretation of Scripture, some forty years ago, there was endless talk about Hellenism, Mystery cults and Gnosticism; but it has all died down and instead we can see the roots not only of

21

Pauline, but of Johannine theology in the Jerusalem of the Pharisees, in Galilee and Qumrân (or wherever the Essene settlements may have been) and in a Judaism that was being spiritually rejuvenated. We can sometimes almost seize the transformations and the links in our hands. We can see Jesus himself taking up the feelings and the spiritual attitudes of his *milieu*, and filling what exists with an entirely new spirit. In prayer and contemplation, the Christian soul can feel what the Jewish soul felt: and that does not merely call for a sort of psychological intuition or a quickened historical sense that enables one to reach a better understanding of the Jewish element. It has a precise theological sense. It means that the conclusions of modern biblical scholarship coincide with the expression of St Paul about the sap and the holy root. The historical knowledge and experience of the Jewish situation as it was—which we Christians can enter into and assimilate by making the effort and the study involved, and using a little imagination—can be seen to converge upon and coincide with a more mysterious and inward experience: the memory of all that is oldest in us, and to which we remain related, that rises up within us, and is nothing else but the faith of Abraham which St Paul and Buber speak of in a curiously dissonant harmony.

St Paul sets out to show that Jew and Gentile, Old and New Covenant, meet in the faith of Abraham. Buber would like to show that they are fundamentally divided in that faith. But whatever the truth may be about the 'two forms of faith' that Buber presupposes (and we shall have to return to the subject), both St Paul and Buber are agreed that the faith of Abraham is not only the true faith in the sense of being the prototype of faith, but that it is God's intervention in history, the foundation to which every believer must attach himself.

22

Why is it then that the faith of Abraham, as it comes to us in the testimony of Buber, does not come to us with the same tone as the original? And why do we close our minds to an experience which seems strange to us Gentile Christians, and refuse to accept something into our Christian memory which is older than Christianity, and that we have, after all, to listen to with the same respect with which the first Christians, and indeed Christ himself, listened to the living voice of tradition? Using the Rosenzweig and Buber translation of the Bible, we can catch something of the tones and over-tones which the Jewish ear heard in the word of God. We can renew and extend the sense of awe which Hammann and Herder felt at the sound of the original words. And in addition to the Bible itself, there are Buber's interpretative works: *Abraham* (1955), *Moses* (1944 and 1952), *Judges* (in *The Kingdom of God* 1932, 1935, 1956) and the *Prophets* (in *The Faith of the Prophets* 1950), all of which explain and interpret the Bible in a purely inward and Jewish sense, and in doing so draw attention to the line of demarcation with Christianity.

If we disregard the inadequacies of historical interpretation, then the common link between the Jewish and the Christian understanding of faith reveals the following law: There can be no Christianity (whether it be the usual Gentile Christianity or a Jewish Christianity) which is not, *a priori* and inwardly, related in a deeply sympathetic manner to the 'holy tree', as the branch is related to the root. Christianity is only the fullness if it is the fulfilment of something . . . But Christianity, in so far as it understands itself as distinct from Judaism, cannot simply concede the possibility that post-Christian Judaism can have a reciprocal relationship of feeling: Judaism *must* inevitably regard Christianity as

23

different, as foreign, and consequently it cannot help but think in terms of 'the two forms of faith'. At the very most, and making the greatest effort to come to meet us, the Jew can either recognise himself again in the Christian thing, or regard it as something essentially foreign to him, or what is more probable, see it as a mixture of both, as something which is at once his own and foreign to him. That is the attitude which Buber took up from the very first, expressing himself in somewhat vehement language in his earliest lectures, and subsequently in milder terms which left the substance of what he had to say unchanged.

'To those who only recently advised us to try to "feel" and sympathise with Christianity,' Buber wrote, 'we may perhaps reply that the creative element in Christianity is not Christian but Judaic, so that there is no *need* for us to "feel" with it; all we have to do is to recognise it within us and take possession of it, for we bear it irrevocably within us. And on the other hand, everything in Christianity that is uncreative is not Judaic, but is compounded of a thousand rites and dogmas, and—speaking as Jews and as men—we have *no intention* of trying to adjust our feelings to it.' (5) The protest against the tendency of Judaism to harden into a ceremonial law, particularly as it occurred among the Essenes, led to a deeper and more spiritual understanding of tradition. It was then 'that the movement which arose in those separate communities crystallised in the nation and kindled the spiritual revolution which is nowadays wrongly and misleadingly called primitive Christianity; it could, with more justice, and should be called primitive Judaism, though not in an historical sense, for it is much closer to Judaism than to what is nowadays called Christianity.' (6)

Buber proves his thesis by pointing to the fact that

Christianity always has to call on Judaism in order to be itself and to renew itself, whereas the contrary is in no sense true. 'The vitality and power of Christ's message consists in the old Jewish demand for an unconditional decision which transforms man and raises him into the Kingdom of God. That has always been the driving power of Christianity, the power to which it always resorts when it wants to rejuvenate itself.' (7) In reserved but expressive terms, Buber points out what an anti-Jewish Christianity leads to—in Germany for instance: it leads directly from the fine liberalism of Harnack to Auschwitz. (8) In general the thesis is correct, though not perhaps for quite the reasons which Buber puts forward: the great renaissances of Christianity have always sprung from the spirit of imitation or following which may certainly be described as the spirit of Abraham and of the Prophets, but which is also quite explicitly the spirit of the following of Christ, the God-man, as may easily be seen from the examples of St Anthony, St Bernard, St Francis or St Ignatius. And as for Luther, who burnt St James's Epistle 'of straw', his message of good tidings is most definitely that of St Paul, which Buber in his turn handles none too gently. All these renewals are undoubtedly a return to the kindling fire of 'the personal', to personal religion, but equally they are always a return to personal religion in its Christian form— the 'I am' texts of Jesus—which remain unacceptable to Buber.

On the other hand, the complementary notion that the decisive outlines of Christianity are already visible in Judaism, and that Judaism reflecting upon itself can recognise itself in them, is naturally entirely acceptable to the Christian. The Fathers of the Church after all have repeatedly expressed the view in various forms that the Old

Covenant is a preamble to the New, and even contains the introduction to the Incarnation, and that the word of the Father moves step by step through the figures of the Old Covenant as part of the economy of salvation, so that the Theophanies and the Angels of Jahweh are to be interpreted with reference to the Son of Man. Taking into consideration all that has been said of the historical character and situation of the word of revelation, and the fact that it was in a sense brought forth with the collaboration of the People, believing, praying and responding, then it is perfectly acceptable from a Christian point of view to maintain that from the beginning Judaism displays a Christian form or structure that becomes progressively more apparent. The path which that development took leads from the pure faith of Abraham, the source and origin, which can be seen shining through historically in the words of Gideon, so carefully stressed by Buber (Judges 8, 22) (9), and from the oldest songs extant, such as that of Deborah, down through the Law and the cult, the Kingdom and the Priesthood, to the time when all those forms and husks were broken, and finally leads to the pure suffering in which Jeremias, Job, and the Servant of the Lord in Isaiah are held, as it were, imprisoned. For the people as a whole, as well as for its representative individuals, that movement leads on to an increasingly definite Christological form. For there are two realities within it which converge and meet and are increasingly merged one in the other: Man, who orders his life, his whole existence, upon the real and living word that dominates everything in him, to the point at which he is ultimately 'taken up' into the Word, and bears witness to it with his life and in his blood—and the Word of God, that speaks less and less from outside, from above, and by degrees becomes the language of existence, in the sense that it uses

26

the whole of existence in order to speak at once more directly, more concretely and more intelligibly to man.

These two aspects are so intimately connected in Judaism, where the first presupposes the existence of the second, that the temptation, understandably enough, is to allow the 'Christological factor' in the Old Testament to suffice in itself —with the result that it seems possible to dispense with the necessity of a break-through, of a thorough-going trans-cendence that opens the way to a new level. And yet Israel knows that it cannot claim parity with the promised figure of the Messiah, or claim to exist on the same level as a truly vicarious suffering, not even in the extreme suffering of its millenary exile. For otherwise there would be nothing to wait for. Israel in fact remains expecting an indefinite future, and, while its whole structure is messianic, it is not the Messiah. That is the great mystery which, because it is unfathomable, confers upon the existence of Israel a strange and awe-inspiring character. (10) The reality of faith, the 'Christo-logical form', only reveals itself to faith. 'The unity of race and community of faith, which is unique in Israel, is not just an empirical fact, nor is it simply its special destiny; it is the point at which the divine touches the human.' (11)

It is, moreover, very difficult for the Christian to make out how far a believing Jew, reflecting upon his faith, can penetrate into the New Testament and the Christological structure of his people, past and present. Christ said that Abraham, the father of the faith, rejoiced to see his day (the day of the Messiah), 'he saw it, and was glad' (Jn. 8, 56). It may be that Jesus introduced an explanatory, contem-porary, apocalyptical factor into Abraham's prophetic vision (12); what is meant, undoubtedly, is that Abraham embraced the fulfilment of what had been promised to him in his faith, in the same way that longing for a joy to come embraces the joy, and that the fact that Abraham did thus embrace the fulfilment implied knowledge and vision. This is all the more true since what was seen was a vision in the fullest sense, as indeed the reply of the Jews makes clear; 'Thou art not yet fifty years old and wouldest have seen Abraham?'—quite independently of whether they understood or misunderstood the context of the words.

But is this anticipation of the fulfilment possible to a believing, post-Christian Jew who *bona fide* rejects the fulfilment of Christ? Are we obliged, as Buber once put it, to call the Jew's reflection upon the spiritual nature of his own people an experience, not a matter of faith but simply of experience? If that were so one would surely have to conclude that Israel had lost its sense of the transcendent, and had come to rest in itself. The more conscious that refusal became, the more strange, external and ultimately unintelligible would the fulfilment be to the Jew, understood from a Christian point of view. This is, in fact, the source of Buber's conception of the various historical origins of religions, a theory which stands out very unexpectedly in an intellectual world which is in other respects so open and so ready to communicate: 'Religions,' he writes, in his answer to Panwitz, 'are the buildings into which the spirit of man is directed so that it should not break out and burst his world asunder. Each of them originates in a particular revelation and its object is to do away with every form of differentiation and particularity. . . That is why it is always a senseless undertaking for a man to allot praise and blame when comparing his own with another religion: his own Temple building, experienced from the inner courtyard, is then compared with the external aspect of a strange one as seen by an attentive observer.' (13)

'We can recognise what another man confesses as being the reality of his faith, though it is contrary to our existence and our knowledge of being, and we can recognise it as a mystery,' he writes to Karl Ludwig Schmidt; 'we are not in a position to pass judgment upon its meaning because we do not know it from within in the same way that we know *ourselves* from within.' (14)

That gesture of refusal, as will be seen, is not Buber's last word on the relation between Judaism and Christianity—nor do we take it as such, but simply as an expression of the fact that the Jew is estranged from the Christian thing, while the Christian—in spite of profound ignorance of post-Christian Judaism—is not estranged in the same sense from Judaism.

CHAPTER THREE

The Prophetic Principle

JUDAISM is a religion which has no central, institutional authority from which one can learn how it understands itself. From the very outset one must, therefore, be prepared for a variety of sometimes conflicting interpretations, and Judaism as often as not reveals its strength in the fact that these constantly renewed differences of opinion on fundamental questions have always been, and still are, held together by an undiminished vitality and dynamism. The principle that holds everything together is neither a doctrine nor an authority nor even a secular government, but the People; and for that reason a schism is impossible. It is therefore possible for parties which, given their constitution, would have gone irreparably or almost hopelessly asunder in the Catholic framework, to be drawn together again within the Jewish framework and formed into a new whole by that centre which is the People.

Martin Buber was in many ways predestined to play a unifying role of that kind. He was born on February 8, 1878, in Vienna, and was taken 'in his third year . . . into the house of his grandparents who lived in Lemberg. Salomon Buber was one of the great figures of the Haskala (the Jewish enlightenment), a prominent member of the Jewish *haute bourgeoisie*, who were rising in the social scale. . . He was a con-

siderable scholar, and a student of the Madrash. Martin
Buber lived in his house until he was fourteen years old,
receiving a solid grounding in the Bible. . . There he found
the atmosphere and traditions of life and the intellectual
climate of the Haskala at their best.' (1) But even at that time
Buber had already discovered Hassidism, in a late and
decadent form it is true, which prompted him to begin
searching for the original source of the movement. As a
university student, he first saw the world in Vienna, and there
for the first time came in contact with the realms of art and
literature. His earliest enthusiasm was Nietzsche, and for a
time he succumbed to the spell, though he soon turned to the
study of mysticism.

It was in the summer of 1898, in Berlin, that Buber met the
two men who were to influence him decisively: Simmel,
whose lectures he attended, while also attending those of
Dilthey; and Theodor Herzl, an attractive personality, who
was one of the originators of the Zionist movement that was
to mean so much in Buber's life. Those were to be the
formative influences in his intellectual development; both his
thought and his life were in fact largely determined by
Simmel's 'Philosophy of Life', and by the dynamism of the
Zionist movement. There was, however, a long road to
traverse before Buber's point of view could mature and un-
fold. The study of Hassidism occupied him from 1905 to 1908,
(2) and later still, from 1919 on, there was his long and
enriching experience of the personalist philosophy. (3)
Finally, in 1930, there was the decisive period when, through
his friendship with the translator of the Bible, Franz Rosenzweig, Buber encountered the absolute demand of the word
in Scripture.

Everything subsequent in his development, however,

crystallised round the poles of Simmel's philosophy and Zionism. Much that was fundamental was, in fact, corrected or improved—for example, the statement that God was a projection of the soul of the people, or mankind's aspiration towards unity—though as he says in the Preface to the Collected Edition of *Lectures on Judaism* where the modifications are made, the corrections only implied 'a clarification and not a conversion'. (4) For Buber was already steeped in Simmel's *Lebensphilosophie*—which could easily accommodate Dilthey's typology—at the time when his enthusiasm for Zionism was first aroused, and the way opened to the method to which he seemed predestined from youth up.

Buber's method is one of ruthless simplification and clarification in which everything superfluous or inessential is mercilessly swept aside—everything that had accumulated during the centuries, everything decadent and distorted: a method of *reduction*, reducing everything to essentials, and which does not falter on the threshold of the Old Testament, but makes use of the whole apparatus of modern biblical scholarship to break through to the kernel and to uncover the source, in order to display it alone as the driving power and inspiration of the whole. There is bitter irony in the way in which Buber goes on to show that those outside Judaism, and even 'Jews of our day, and those among them who are most zealous in their search for the truth' (5), fail utterly, for the most part, to recognise the unity of Judaism, so that disillusioned by the 'conventional Christian' picture of their faith, they turn to Christianity—and he instances Bergson and Simone Weil. The inexorable consistency of his method enables Buber to break down the rigid opposition between traditional and orthodox Judaism, by refusing to concern himself with anything but the essential principle.

His first lectures demolish the tenaciously defended card-house of Talmudism, by interpreting and understanding the words and expressions and prohibitions accepted as absolute in relative terms, and as the expression of a religious attitude. There are Jews to this day who cannot get over the disappearance of the Temple, although there were circles, such as that from which Jesus came, which had already turned away from the formalities of the Temple ceremonies of their time, and had gone beyond them. (6) Moreover, who could seriously wish to reintroduce slaughtering regulations that obtained in the old Temple, and which were tolerable and suitable 'at a time when the relation to God was very naïve', but that had already been criticised by the prophets and had lasted too long when they were forcibly terminated? The priesthood as a whole, consequently, ceases to have any function and becomes superfluous, and could not be restored; though Buber does not fail to emphasise the inward problem which this raises. The petrifaction of Sacrifice, Scriptures and Tradition proceeds simultaneously (7); religions degenerate into a 'swarming hive of formulae'. For Religion, whatever its form, only has meaning and point if it helps to make the immediate, free and personal gesture of the religious man more adequate and more expressive. One can of course pour the content of experienced religion into propositions and call them 'dogmas', but the dogma remains a secondary matter. The primary thing is the religious life of Judaism . . . 'the recollection and expectation of a precise situation in concrete history: the encounter of God and mankind. Everything that is affirmed in the abstract or in the third person about the Divine, everything that goes beyond the sphere of "I and

Thou" is a construction, a projection on the conceptual plane that is always felt as inessential but unavoidable.' (8) Buber affirms a living 'religiosity' which generates a living expression, a living law and custom; and he utterly repudiates 'religion', no longer quickened by feeling, that hardens into ritualism and dogmatism. The religious by-products of Rabbinism and Rationalism, and those who 'toyed with the crowned corpse of the law', crippled the free growth of Judaism as effectually as the moral and political persecutions of the Jews in Christendom. The law is important but only in so far as it leads mankind itself to become the Thora. (9)

To take one example, the old biblical prohibition to make an image of God must be interpreted in the light of Jewish religiosity; its purpose simply cannot have been to hinder and curb the artistic development of the people, so that the Temple of Solomon, the sanctuary of their cult, had to be designed by foreign craftsmen; but to keep alive the invisible relation of God to his people. Buber defends a Jewish art because he interprets Judaism, to a very large extent, in terms of the incarnation of the spirit, and the 'sacramentalising' of the whole of existence in the spirit of the encounter with God. He therefore defends the presence of myths in Holy Scripture, because myth (both in the broad sense of a concrete symbol of the spiritual, and also in the narrower sense of a narrative giving concrete form to the encounter with the divine) corresponds with and is indispensable to human religiosity. 'The Jews of antiquity cannot narrate except in terms of myth.' (10) That is to say, Buber accepts and defends the body of thought that is common to the romantic movement and modern psychology, and that stresses the significance of the myth-making faculty of the creative imagination, particularly at early periods, when word and image are still powerfully influenced by racial experience. (11) Not even his arguments with Jung prevented Buber from holding fast to these ideas which he developed in his youth.

The forms that hardened one after another into rigidity did so because they had become partitions sealing off the fluid, personal, 'I-Thou' relationship which is that of the Covenant between the Lord and his people, and these forms are rejected, one after another. What remains, where Buber is concerned, is mankind's affirmation of the unconditional presence of God, first of all that of the individual, Abraham's, then that of the tribe, and after the days of Moses that of the people. It is the *presence* of God that is the unconditional, the revelation—not some teaching about the 'essence of God'. Buber is never tired of repeating that a hellenistic interpretation of Ex. 3, 14, 'I am who am', is a complete falsification of the whole Judaic principle, because it leads on to a theology instead of to the promise that God will lead his people in the real historical situation—and he translates the phrase: 'I shall be as I shall be.'

The original relation of those called (whether individual or people) to the one who calls is a relationship of unqualified trust and faithfulness which assumes responsibility and accepts service, and with Abraham in mind it can be called 'faith'; but Buber, more especially in his early works, suspects the word because, to him, Abraham's faith, rightly understood, has little or nothing to do with faith as it appears in the theology of St Paul: which is to say, the contrary of 'the works of the law', belief in an extraneous justification following upon the work and grace of Christ. Jewish faith, on the contrary, is an active, efficacious confidence and trust; at bottom it is action, the realisation or actualisation of the very

35

centre of the person, and in so far as the person has turned away and is lost, it implies return and conversion. (12) The call, in that perspective, is the ever-new, spontaneous event of prophecy which is in no sense derivative, and cannot be foreseen or calculated.

To Buber, therefore, Judaism is coincident with a vital prophetic tradition. That is the simple basic theme of all his sometimes minute interpretations of Scripture. Even the founder Abraham—the visionary, the man of prayer who intercedes for others—must be understood in that light. He is the first to be 'singled out' as are all those who were called after him; and we can see from his case that 'the prophetic existence is as old as Israel'. (13) This becomes even more striking in the case of Moses, whose mission shows that 'he was obviously called as a *Nabi*, as a prophet'. But that does not mean to say that Moses was only a *Nabi*, simply that the task in the service of which he returned to Egypt is essentially related to the task as it was subsequently narrated and interpreted by the 'sages' of Israel already historically secure in their knowledge. When Hosea, one of the earliest of the prophetic writers declares 'and by a prophet the Lord brought Israel out of Egypt' (12, 13), he certainly does not mean that Moses was only one of the *Nebiim*, but that he fulfilled his task as a *Nabi*. Prophecy does not consist primarily in an ecstatic experience, for 'that would imply shifting the centre of gravity from the people and its actions to the personal sphere of the life of faith'; nor does it consist in miraculous deeds, 'such as are told of Elijah and in particular of Elisha—for that would mean exchanging history for a legend'. 'On the contrary, the essential thing that concerns us here can only be the *historical* situation, repeated again and again from Samuel to Jeremias, in which the *Nabi* time and again breaks into history and acts historically; that is the great historical refrain of Israel: Prophet against King. What this image offers is neither mythology nor stylised history, but the flesh and blood of history.' (14) The legendary cycle of the plagues of Egypt, for example, is paralleled in the subsequent threats of the prophets, which are produced in the same form: as alternatives. Buber's great three-volume work *Das Kommende*, of which the first (and so far the only) volume, *The Kingdom of God*, deals with the period of the Judges, develops the same thesis on a new plan (which may be completed by referring to the more general book, *The Faith of the Prophets*). The Judges represent the historically improbable, the Utopian element, and yet they are the perfect expression of the Lordship of JHWH over Israel. That principle repeatedly becomes actual in those called by the spirit and at the free disposal of the Lord of the Covenant; they administer in the name and the place of God, but do not put trust in any institutional or decreed authority whether temporal or spiritual. 'And Gideon said to them: I will not rule over you, neither shall my son rule over you, but the Lord shall rule over you.' (Judges 8, 23.) Gideon's words indicate the climate of the whole period which is characterised by the fact that the priestly office is hereditary while the political is not. The former is wholly charismatic. (15) However the analogies suggested by the Bedouin may be interpreted, they do not suffice to explain the unique paradox of the radical and literal theocracy that existed in Israel, in which 'for the first time faith is freed from magic' and the charisma of election remains in the hands of God who (as may be seen from Saul) can withdraw it. The prophetic role that comes to the fore under the last Judge, Samuel, and the first King, Saul, must have developed under the Judges, and Buber sees in it 'the community spread over the land and fighting for the Lord, which brought forth the Judges and maintained them in being'. (16) 'Tradition in the era before David . . . ignores any form of charisma except that of the prophet; even the Judges, like Gideon and Jephta, even the fanatics like Samson, must first of all become prophets, *Nebiim.*' (17)

A crisis is unavoidable, precipitated by the political organism itself, which is in search of stability. It is none other than Samuel, the blameless one, who makes his very different sons his successors; and the representatives of the people, who beg him instead for an institutional Kingdom are simply following his lead and going a step further. But what King could resist the temptation to power, and where Israel is concerned that means the temptation to exchange the 'charismatic' leadership of God in the political order for the independent authority of a Ruler who administers power with the competence of the specialist. It is the political institution that makes the charismatic representative of God's sovereignty into a 'worldly' ruler, and it is only after that dangerous secularisation has taken place that the twofold opposition to the Kingship appears: a well-established 'spiritual' institution, the priestly office with its hierarchy devoted in the main to the Court; and the tradition of the prophetic office, powerless from a worldly point of view, that cannot do otherwise than adopt a critical attitude to the twofold institution of Kingship and Priesthood. Their protest leads the prophets into the suffering which is their destiny, and that is the certain proof of the unique, utopian character of the Jewish charismatic theocracy—unique from a worldly point of view —and which from a purely political standpoint leads in the end *ad absurdum*, but is always rejuvenated and reconstituted by the same power, the martyrdom of the prophets. As long

as that source remains fresh and alive, both love and
obedience, decision in the instant and loyalty in time converge and coincide; and the disruptive tendency that leads
into a dualism where sacred and profane are divorced can
always be halted and the harm repaired. Israel should know
that it cannot divide things in that way, that everything
belonging to the profane sphere, family, community, State,
politics and economics, must be subject to the realm and
power of faith and receive its form from them.

The fact that the centre of gravity of Israel's religion, from
the days of Abraham to the Exile, lies in the prophetic
principle, inevitably reduces the post-exile period to the
position of a postscript of minor importance. The transition
which then occurred, from prophecy to apocalypse, means,
according to Buber, a transition from a religious experience
rooted in historical decision (where it depends upon man's
choice whether the divine threat is put into execution or not),
to a vision of the beyond, a complete image of the future
course of history which has still to be unveiled, and so of a
world in which man does not have to choose and is not called
upon to make a decision. The apocalyptic element that
emerges with Ezekiel, and is triumphant in Daniel and the
pre-Christian apocalyptic books is not, in his view, Jewish at
all, but Iranian in origin, and Christianity's acceptance of the
principle disposes it from the first to be a religion lacking in
unity.

As has already been said, that argument takes Buber
beyond Orthodoxy and Liberalism, Eastern and Western
Judaism, and beyond the spirit of the Synagogue and the
Zionist movement. By his origins and upbringing, indeed, he
understood and embraced both sides. But while it would
appear impossible in Christendom to embrace Catholicism

and Protestantism, or Orthodox and Liberal Protestantism from a single standpoint, it would really seem that in this case the special character of Judaism makes it possible to preserve the unity. And since this possibility of unity is not only at the source of Judaism, but equally of everything Christian, it enables Buber to look down like a sort of judge upon the interplay of differences among Christians, and to allot praise and blame in the light of that source. The Catholic Church would then be right to stress an active conversion and works in faith, as they are emphasised in the Epistle of St James, and also, for example, in emphasising a living tradition as opposed to the written word alone; whereas Protestantism is fundamentally more right when it volatilises the elements which the Catholic Church has made absolute: Dogma, obligatory sacraments, the hierarchical institution and obedience to the Church. The Protestant is right to keep everything fluid in order to secure a purely personal attitude. Both, however, are profoundly wrong when they accept the Pauline stigmatisation of faithfulness to the Covenant of Sinai—as though the Law could not be obeyed, as though God only wanted to demonstrate to man through the Covenant that he was not fit for the Covenant! For in that case they commit themselves to a sort of gnostic crypto-marcionism.

In criticism of Buber's method of 'reduction', it could be said that it bears rather too plainly the stamp of its age. It could never have assumed so radical a form were it not for the *Lebensphilosophie*, seen at its best in those who came after Nietzsche, such as Bergson, and as expressed by Simmel. At the time when he was writing *The Holy Way* and some of his finest Addresses, such as *Cheruth*, one can hear the unmistakable tonality and dynamism of 'the philosophy of life'. Life gives birth to the form in which it expresses itself, but sooner or later the form petrifies, and then life reveals its power in the fact that it overflows the form, whatever it may be. The doctrine can be expressed in very balanced form, as both Bergson and Simmel have demonstrated, and although it was sharply criticised by the Marburg school, in fact it only transferred the unyielding system of 'reduction', which dominated the neo-Kantian school, from the ethical field to a different plane, reducing anything objective to thought and idea, and to the absolute of an ethical demand which could not be expressed in the formal demand, and still less in a single action. It was a dynamic system of reduction which explained everything in terms of spirit and idea and life, on the higher or on a lower plane: and finally, it embraced both simultaneously in Scheler's later dualistic work which derives from Bergson's, and for a time ran parallel to that of Husserl—until in the end Scheler broke through to the absolute and personal encounter of love—only to end with a tragic yet heroic discord between idea and instinct. And lastly, there is the influence of the socialist manifestos and doctrine which must not be overlooked; they transposed Hegel's dialectical movement of history into action and decision, and gave Hegel's meaning a very concrete and messianic twist. It was in the context of all these movements that the Jewish movement unfolded, and the young Buber tried to discover the essential qualities of Judaism in terms of a philosophical anthropology.

At one moment he saw Israel as the mediator between East and West: rooted in the East, but looking out on to the Mediterranean from its home in Palestine, on to the birthplace of the West with which it shared the instinct to realise its aspirations. Jerusalem is spiritually as well as geographically 'the gateway of the nations, the eternal traffic centre of East and West'. (18) Then again he sees the Jew as the most tragic of all figures, an ambivalent, dualistic man, deeply divided against himself, and therefore born to seek unity in its highest forms. The Jew is the representative man, and his mutability goes to the very heart of his being. In him man's struggle takes on an exemplary character. (19) But however the image is illuminated, the dynamic movement remains the same, and the Jew appears at the very centre of human existence which he makes manifest and prefigures. Jewish theology is philosophy made manifest. This is not altered by the fact that Buber subsequently toned down the mystical and monistic vitalism of his early formulae when he adopted a form of personalism which is much closer to biblical realism (down to the latest forms of personalism in *Urdistanz und Beziehung* which, as can be seen from the title, discards the exaggerations of his youth and explicitly rejects the fluid unification which blurs the difference between God and creature): nor is his view fundamentally changed if personalism is regarded as resting upon the prophetic principle, the truly human encounter in the absolute spirit.

But the objection that Buber's thought is too deeply influenced and determined by the thought of his age is really a minor matter, since in fact the movement of his thought as a whole is the fruit of Jewish thinkers and men of action: the proletarian socialism of Marx and Engels, the Marburg school led by Hermann Cohen, and the *Lebensphilosophie* of Bergson, Simmel and Scheler. For all these men provided intellectual clothing for a specifically Jewish attitude or point of view, and Buber was surely right to allow himself to be carried along by them until he reached his own original destination. It was also surely worth while attempting to apply the Jewish principle thus gained to Christianity defined in its primitive form and message—the Sermon on the Mount—and to test its originality and its subsequent forms in that light. It would indeed have been very strange if the climate of the period had not made itself felt: perhaps one could describe it, by contrast with the reserve and decorum of the Old Testament, where the expropriation of the Land is not 'expansion', as having the stigma of Western activism, and more precisely, a restless revolutionary impulse. The old prophets are radical, but one could not describe them as radical revolutionaries.

Martin Buber must have met Gustav Landauer, the practician and theorist of endemic spiritual revolution, some time before 1900, and he subsequently quotes from the revolutionary book which he prompted Landauer to write in 1907. The sentence is interesting in its bearing on Buber's interpretation of the Old Testament: 'The image and feeling of a positive union brought about by the unifying character of love, which is always a power, invariably awakens or re-awakens the fire, enthusiasm and the fraternity of these aggressive movements; and but for those transitional periods of regeneration we could not live on and should certainly founder.' (20) But there are other aspects of the question which are not so clear: there is the basic impulse of Zionism to bring about the reunification of the dispersed Jews, and a dissatisfaction with any established form once it is attained— a tendency that was taken up and sharpened by Western Jewry when it transformed the dynamism of Fichte and Hegel into a *Weltanschauung*: all these elements make one wonder whether Buber's schematised presentation and 'reduction' of the essence of the Old Testament events really goes to the bottom of the matter. That question will have to be asked in more precise form before the end of this inquiry, but for the moment we can be content to circumscribe our suspicions.

The Old Covenant can only be reduced to a single principle, the prophetic principle as Buber understands it (though widened and elucidated by the sacramental principle which remains to be considered), by following the method of *regression* which Buber himself adopts in interpreting Old Testament history: that is, by working back from the hopelessly corrupt forms of the post-exile period to a classical age of prophecy, which is itself the result of a fundamental deviation from the Judaic norm, produced by replacing the sovereignty of God, the theocracy, by a human institution, the Kings, and then tracing the prophetic principle back to the fully normative period before institutional petrifaction set in, when the theocratic idea, in spite of its historical inadequacy was, from time to time, manifested in a pure form. Buber is well aware of all that is lost in the process of regression: nothing less, indeed, than the forward, progressive movement of Jewish history, which means to say the prehistory of everything Buber utterly rejects in its immanent but none the less Judaic form and that comes to light in the Pauline interpretation of Faith and Law. But Buber does not attempt to deceive himself—or us. The charismatic theocracy which his regressive method reveals as the ideal phase contains the seed of the tragic dualism to come. It leads on to the decadent forms of the later periods of the history of Israel. 'A theocracy, radically interpreted, is a risk . . . which inevitably leads on to a crisis in which the contradictions latent in every race explode. But those who side in the struggle with God's sovereignty, and against the sovereignty of "History" will

44

experience therein an awe-inspiring eschatological view.' (21) The risk of a theocracy breaks down on the inertia of the whole people and throws the individual, isolated by nature, into relief, so that the individual is forced into opposition to the masses, to all those who, being of the masses, naturally choose the easier path and prefer to become part of the institution. And that is to recognise that if the revelation of God does not only involve the individual, but calls a whole people into its service, it must be tragic, and is bound to manifest this tragic aspect as history unfolds. And that is the point at which Buber's anger against St Paul rebounds.

We—and 'we' means the Christian people in this case— are not trying to take advantage of that tragic interpretation of Israel's history in order to convert it. In company with Israel, we wish to recognise the justice of the idea and its whole import. In Christian apologetics, the institutional element in religion is defended on two grounds: first of all 'because of the created form of human nature, whose characteristic it is to reach the spiritual through the sensual'; and secondly on the ground that because man has sinned 'he is falsely related to corporeal things.' (22) But we have still to consider how the two grounds are related to one another. Can one simply isolate the first from the second, or should they not rather be taken together as one, and the tension between them regarded as an expression of the human condition in history? That does not mean that we must concede the institutional element the same rank as the prophetic element, resigning ourselves to the fact that the world is what it is; or by naïvely excluding the second reason, treat the people of God as though they were in all things like any other purely human community. But it does mean that we must make the same effort to find salvation that Buber undertakes in his historical regression, and with the same good-will try to understand the original Covenant and the Kingdom of God as the truth and to live that truth, allowing ourselves to be sufficiently humbled in order to admit that salvation can only be attained by the healing ways decreed by God for our tragic falls. Otherwise there is a grave danger that the freely-given and prayerful prophecy of the Old Testament be transformed into something very different, some modern form of Judaism, something man can 'acquire', unrelated to prayer and sooner or later unrelated to God, dialectical, moralistic and in one sense or another progressive. Prophecy after all, is not a 'principle' at all if it implies a solid basis rooted in human nature. Prophecy is a gift at God's disposal, and though one may lament the fact that 'the signs have ceased' or that 'there is now no prophet' (Ps. 73, 9), it would be wrong to reproach God or to read into their absence an unambiguous sign of guilt. It may well be that the period of darkness, when God is eclipsed, which none of the prophets escaped—neither Abraham nor Moses nor Elias—may become the source of a new experience of God and of the divine message of suffering for the People, just as it did for the prophets. But the inescapable destiny of being the People of God is among the burdens which it has to bear, and it will never be able to determine how great is the weight of its own sins and how great the burden of grace. No one who reads attentively can fail to perceive that the giving of the Keys to Peter is closely related to the promise of suffering. Whether from a Jewish or a Christian point of view, there is no choice but to recognise that the institutional element (to which the Scriptures themselves belong) always needs to be made transparent through the power of prayer and a believing heart, in

46

order that the charismatic element should be seen: that is the purpose of the institution sanctioned and placed upon us by the hand of God in order to strengthen us and weaken us, uplifting and humbling man at the same time, so as to place him once again in his right and original relation to God.

The Institution always needs to be made Transparent through the power of prayer and a believing heart.

CHAPTER FOUR

The Sacramental Principle

As WE see it in the Bible, in all its reality, the prophetic principle contains what, for the sake of clarity, we shall call an independent second principle, for it derives from the first. The truth of this can, to a great extent, be seen from what has already been said. In perfect accord with his method of 'reduction', Buber presents an image of man of great simplicity: man in pure faith and confidence before God. Man's simplicity, however, is also his *unity*, as the words of Jesus testify: 'If thy eye be single, thy whole body shall be lightsome.' (Mt. 6, 22). Body, in this context, embraces the whole of man's physical and earthly life, private as well as public, and embraces the political and sociological sphere. That embodiment, which always safeguarded the prophetic principle from going astray or from becoming destructive, is the second privilege conferred upon Israel and is its most important dowry: Jewry ultimately means the unity of religion and the body politic. Unity, in Israel, is not the ideal, cosmic, mystical unity dreamed of by the highest representatives of other religions, which cannot be conceived apart from a search for the spiritual and leaves the particular and the concrete far behind; on the contrary, it is grounded in the marriage of a particular man with a particular place on earth, of an Adam and an Adama, of a personal and a national spirit, with this earth. It is neither physical nor 'earthy' but a spiritual marriage founded upon spirit: the land receives a people that is obedient and follows God's leadership; the rains come and the crops ripen—while the disobedient are driven out of the Land itself and are banished. In that way alone it is at the same time both human and divine: it is human because man is always an individual and can only be formed of one 'material'; divine because the sacred marriage of spiritual and material is linked to a condition: the bond of obedience to the Covenant. The dualism of body and spirit, people and country, religion and the *polis* (with its politics) is invariably a sign of a deep disobedience. In so far as that dualism is revealed in even more tragic forms in the history of Israel, Buber strives with all his might, swimming against the tide of history, to return to the source of salvation at once all-inclusive, but relative. For, from a Jewish point of view, the apocalyptic attitude which developed during the Exile, creating its vision of the beyond on the ruins of the present, can hardly be taken seriously. But, in spite of all his efforts, the dichotomy reappears at the very heart of prophecy in its classical form. The tragic opposition between the powerless spirituality of the prophet and the unspiritual power of the Kings and the institutional priesthood can only be explained as the result of an inward unrest. From a religious point of view, salvation is only found in the era before the Kingdom, in the days of the Judges with their charismatic politics and that legendary origin which is nevertheless so very clearly expressed by the legend: the story of how People and Land are joined by grace. Everything that comes later, all the subsequent stages and phases continually hark back to that original mystery, and the spirit of Israel centres on it, and is rooted in it. It is a sacrament because the Land was given to the People by the grace of God, and the Land itself works their salvation: it is a sacrament administered as a physical sign of the divine and free efficacy of grace, and it is the grace-given permission for the men who inhabit that abode to labour and make it into the field of expression of their obedience.

Buber has described this mystery from every angle in *Israel and Palestine* (1950). He begins with its biblical foundations and traces it down through the whole history of Israel and on to the present time, demonstrating the vitality of the idea, and finally sketching in briefly how it was completed in Zionism. Among the many fascinating sections of the book is that in which he gives an account of Rabbi Löw's theology of history (1) which interprets the mystery of the Land in the conceptual language of Aristotle and St Thomas. Every aspect of the book vibrates in harmony, the theological and the poetic, the mystical, sociological and political. It is the work of a *Chowew-Zion*, a lover of Zion. For in spite of its semi-nomadic origins and legend, Israel, to Buber, is essentially a nation of peasants. 'Isaac's blessing upon Jacob,' he writes, 'is the blessing of a man who works the land, and Joseph's dream about the sheaves of corn is the dream of a man who lives by the land. The whole of scripture, during the Palestinian period, breathes a deep love of the soil, it is a transfiguration of the cultivation of the soil such as we find among few other peoples. Divine promises and divine threats are almost always delivered in terms of husbandry, and Jesus Sirach expresses a centuries-old feeling when he says that the ploughman keeps the eternal creation alive. Seldom has there been a people so satisfied and so happy in its domicile . . . God was the feudal lord of the Land, his feasts were agricultural feasts and his laws the laws of an agricultural people. Though the prophets might rise to the greatest spiritual heights, they were still rooted in that natural life and they wanted their demands to be realised within the framework of that natural life.' (2) Israel only really became nomadic as a result of the Exile, when it was driven from the Land; and it can only be restored to full health by returning to the Land.

Buber's diagnosis of the illnesses of the Jewish mind is unmerciful. He speaks of the 'dreadful pathological state of our nation throughout its two thousand years of existence' (3) and on another occasion says that 'the intellectuality of the Jew is a tremendous fact, perhaps the most outstanding fact of his racial pathology . . . It is crippled, rigid, sick, twisted, unproductive, unrealistic and inhuman.' (4) Only a return to the Land, to the soil, can bring salvation 'to the sickest of nations' (5) which needs to be wholly re-educated. One of the fruits of its *déracinement* is the attitude of the Jew to money, trade and capitalism; and where that attitude coincides with a religious traditionalism, 'and the religious forms are divorced from their original foundations, they come to terms with the lowest and most depraved forms of capitalism'—and there one finds 'the nadir of present-day Jewry'. (6) Salvation can only come from the Land, even though the whole nation may not be able to live in it. Once the nucleus is healed, health will gradually spread to those who are dispersed throughout the world. Buber takes up and develops this idea, which Achad Haam had taught 'in the spirit of prophetic Judaism' (7), though without giving it adequate theological foundations, and anchors it firmly in the mystery of the Land, of which only one aspect, of course, touches on the mystery of God, while in other respects it is subject to the laws of sociology, pedagogy and political science.

The last chapters of *Paths in Utopia* indicate what a theological sociology and ethics might and should mean to those who have returned to Israel. It could mean refuting that other consequence of Jewish thought in exile, an abstract and ultimately dualistic Marxism, by giving a concrete and practical example of socialism. But this socialism would have to be rooted in the personal sphere, where relations between individuals provide the ethical and religious arena for decisions in the moral order. Then, upon that foundation, it would be possible to take modern society, which is so amorphous and atomistic, and reconstruct it in a genuinely federative sense out of the living web of cells, building the social structure round family, village and group and finally embracing the whole community. Buber looks upon 'the Hebrew co-operative village in Palestine' as 'the one full-scale attempt, whether in the past or in the present, to create a peolpe's co-operative'. That daring undertaking did not collapse, and it is a living example in the sense that the fluid and plastic character of the ideal was preserved. It brought forth a driving power but did not give birth to dogmas or crystallise in a rigid and all-embracing plan; the inner tensions between the Chazulim, the élite, and pioneers of the movement, and the naturally more indolent masses did not threaten the bond which unites them. (8) What is at stake is neither more nor less than the reintegration of God's people, which is to be realised by the rejuvenation of the social programme of the prophets—not in the preponderantly secularised atmosphere of modern socialism, but in the spirit of faith that desires an active correspondence to the grace of the promise.

At this point it becomes necessary to consider what Buber regards as a fundamental factor in the spiritual and intellectual history of Judaism: Hassidism. Although Hassidism emerged in the *déraciné* climate of the Galuth, and what is more remarkable still, weighed down by the legacy of a Kabbalistic dualism and a demoniacal spiritualism, it nevertheless preserved in its ideal the original and healthy attitude of Israel. The aim of the Hassidim, according to Buber, though it was pursued in a naïve manner, was to express in their lives the unity of the spiritual and the secular, and so to bridge the gulf between sacred and profane. In a word, their ideal was a sacramental existence.

The Kabbala, for example, assert that sparks of the divine life have descended into matter and are imprisoned in it. The Hassidim strip the notion of its mythical and pantheistic dress, and retain the kernel of truth: 'Sparks of the divine inhabit all things and beings, and they are offered to man so that in contact with them, he may release and save that divine element. In the final analysis, man's existence in the world is characterised by the fact that things and beings are given to him with that sacramental potentiality ... Man's significance lies in a personal decision, in his readiness to live a sacramental life, to bear his part in the event of salvation. That is what is offered and given to me; and in it God speaks to me and wants an answer from me.' (9) There is no situation which cannot be sanctified by a right intention, a proper attitude, a correct orientation of mind. Nothing, in itself, is evil; and equally nothing, in itself, is pre-sanctified. The right thing religiously speaking is the ordinary everyday thing, not something singled-out in a religious context; and in so far as this is properly done, we collaborate to an incomprehensible degree in the salvation of the world. The core of the Hassidic teaching lies in the personal life of faith 'which helps to build the community—and not, be it noted, a union, a separate Order, cut off from social life and safeguarding an esoteric doctrine divorced from the ordinary life of the world, but on the contrary forming a community of men who remain members of a family, of a class, taking part in the public life of the community, some of them close, others less close, to the Master, but all of them expressing in their own free and public lives the order which they have received from him.' (10) 'God wants everything to be sanctified so that on the Messianic day there will be no distinction between sacred and profane, because everything will have become holy ... and the Thora, being completed, will embrace the whole of life; indeed there will no longer be any form of existence except that which is informed by the Thora, and in which it has become life.' (11) And so (according to Buber) there is nothing evil in itself in the eyes of the Hassid; what is lower and therefore tempts one down, has its place in the whole, and in its right place it will be embraced in the general salvation, which is really union (Jichud) through 'elevation'.

It is worth noting that at this point Buber refers briefly to Freudian psychoanalysis which took up an old Hassidic idea in its theory of 'the sublimation of the libido.' But while 'everything in Freud's theory is confined to the psychical plane', and the sublimation 'takes place inside men', the Hassidic interpretation of the release of the divine spark implies 'an objective event' which takes place between God and the world and even between God and man, whose destiny in the world, whose 'Schechina', helps man to turn to God. (12) Further study of Freud's roots in the Jewish intellectual world would certainly yield interesting results.

Finally, Buber explains the pan-sacramental life of the Hassidim by pointing to the existence of the biblical prophets whose whole existence, physical and spiritual, became an expression and an instrument of divine speech: 'The whole man becomes mouth.' (13) The word 'needs to be completed by attitude and action and the expressive power which is latent in them'. (14) The fact that Hosea marries a harlot and gives his children unholy names ' is a holy action of tremendous seriousness, a sacred drama'. (15) In the light of the biblical conception that man can always be at the call of God, the Hassidic doctrine may also be regarded as a victory over the process which occurs in all historical religions: the tendency to 'set apart the material and the action of the sacrament' is heavily burdened with the temptation to make men 'only feel safe in the purely objective accomplishment of the rite divorced from personal devotion and abandonment, and to look for security in the *opus operatum*, thus avoiding what is envisaged and demanded of the whole man.' (16) Here one sees the ethical and the religious almost coinciding with the sacramental sphere, which is why Buber regards it as the original and primitive Judaic notion primitively expressed in the relation of People to Land.

Where Israel is concerned, the supreme incarnation of the sacred is the Land—exhausting to conquer, and only conquered at the very limit of human endurance, and then again exhausting to cultivate, but at the same time God-given, a pure grace, possessed though only loaned, simultaneously the present and the promise and an ever-new task. In genuine Judaism 'the holiness of work and the holiness of grace are one'. (17)

The Apostles, on the other hand, were fishermen, and one can fish in any waters. Jesus at once saw in their calling the image of their world-wide apostolate. The Jews, on the contrary, cling to the soil, to their own patch of earth. The Church of the Apostles had already cut itself off from the land, and, moreover, ever since the ascension of the risen Christ, had become perfectly indifferent to locality. Its ideal, the *Civitas Dei*, is not of this world, and the Church has its own 'sacred' sacraments which do not coincide with the sacraments of the ordinary everyday situation. Christianity re-established the dualism of sacred and profane, of Church and State, which may perhaps be regarded as a convenient way of avoiding the real task, or if it is in some sense justifiable would still have to be regarded as encouraging that form of escapism. The real task is to be converted and, by realising the faith here and now, make room for the Kingdom of God. The Sermon on the Mount means neither more nor less; 'his gospel message did not reach the nations in its genuine form, but only in a dualistic form'. This dualism is familiar in its most consistent form in the work of St Augustine, and it leads quite logically to the divorce of religion and politics, for in Augustine's thought the sphere of community and state, the assumption that man has to respond to the call with the *whole* of his life, is sacrificed, and the realm of the state is cut off from the Kingdom of God. 'Again and again the imperial conception was invoked in an attempt to overcome that dualism, but always in vain, (18)

There are many reasons, according to Buber, why Christianity can never give itself unreservedly to the worldly task as Judaism sees it. For one thing it is to a certain extent the heir to the late Jewish, or to be more precise, Iranian apocalyptic religious ideas which, by rigidly fixing the ultimate historical decision in the future, clips its own wings. There is also the conception of 'the fullness of time' which, from the start, outstrips and so rules out a completely free future, with the result that the Christian does not really face an open future but simply has to wait in expectation for what has already happened, the return of the saviour who worked the salvation of the whole world and everything in it. For the

Christian the end of time came with the Cross and the Resurrection, and nothing further is to be expected; whereas time in Judaism is not tied to any fixed or central point, and being left to the current which flows on unimpeded, the Jew can strive with all his might towards the End. 'In Christianity the decisive event has already occurred, and from now on it can only be "imitated" . . . whereas in Judaism the decisive event is happening all the time.' (19)

As a result of this characteristic attitude, Judaism is at once a strictly eschatological and secular force in the 'present' world, and its function or calling is to represent the future of mankind in two distinct senses, so that it indicates its theological and absolute aspect, as well as its earthly aspect, in the same way that the Holy Land is both holy and a particular country. That is what confers an 'impossible' breadth and tension upon the Jewish form of existence, transforming the chosen people into a Utopian, sacramental people; it is set as a sign among the nations to remind them that 'heaven and earth' belong together, and then again, by virtue of being a sign and of their sacramental character, they consecrate the world as a whole to that same destiny. Theirs is not an isolated, 'supernatural', existence; for what matters is the soil of Palestine, a soil like any other to cultivate, just as the ploughs and tractors are the same as any others. The 'material' of the sacrament, in scholastic terms, is the soil of Palestine, and that fact gives the sacrament an efficacy in the worldly sphere, which a man belonging to the spiritual Israel, the Church, cannot, obviously, claim to possess.

Buber may therefore be said to interpret the Utopian ideal of Israel, by implication at least, to signify *the identity of the natural and the supernatural*. In doing so he is in the direct line of descent of Chassidic piety, as may be seen from the following quotation. 'I simply cannot believe,' one Rabbi writes, 'that God would confuse and mislead our poor minds with ways that run counter to the movement of nature. It seems to me, rather, that when we say Nature, we mean the created aspect of what happens, and that when we say "miracle" we refer to its revealed aspect . . . "Miracle," to us, means the reception of the eternal revelation. And then, who knows the frontiers of nature—for after all it is God's!' (20) And so the Jew who accepts the rain that falls on the soil of Palestine as an image of grace, and even as grace itself, is quite certain that where God is concerned the distinction which has become so normal to us, between natural and supernatural, 'simply does not exist'. (21) Israel cannot think of itself except as being chosen by God, and in the framework of the Covenant. It is not a naturally identifiable people which was subsequently drawn into the Covenant; its whole existence is dependent upon that 'supernatural' election and mission, which is, however, an earthly, fleshly one. And since Israel is the 'truth' of mankind, and since its task is to bring that truth to light for the whole of mankind through the sacrament of its election, the same thing must also be true of mankind as a whole which, in Holy Scripture, is always seen and understood in relation to Israel. The history of creation is history leading up to Israel, in the same way that the end of history (when God judges the nations), and ultimately everything that lies between beginning and end, leads to Israel. To Israel therefore the subsequent Christian distinction between the natural and the supernatural spheres is utterly foreign; everything natural in Israel is *out of* the supernatural, in the sense that the race, its very blood, is what it is by election, and any divorce between the realms seems unreal.

Buber's interpretation of man and existence is both theological and philosophical, and this follows logically from his method, the 'dialogical principle'. It is also the basic Jewish principle, for in Judaism man can only understand himself face to face with God (and, through God, with his fellow men); it is the principle of humanity which comes to light in the Jew. Buber does, however, recognise a 'basic distinction' between nature and history, nature being the field of God's unchanging and consistent revelation, while history is the field of the free acts of God and man (22), but he can only construct his anthropology on the definite fact of man called before God and placed in that situation. The modern philosophical statement of that identity between natural and supernatural is found in the Personalism of the Jew Max Scheler, whose work betrays his awareness of the fact that he was writing in opposition to the scholasticism of St Thomas. (23) Scheler's personalism is the contemporary expression of the Jewish sacramental principle, in the same way that the vitalistic philosophies of Bergson and Simmel correspond to the prophetic principles. What is typical of Scheler is the way in which the personal equation embraces both extremes, the opposite poles, within the same bracket: both spirit (*deitas*) and instinct; on the one hand an ideality which at one moment becomes explicitly supernatural (*Das Ewige im Menschen*), and on the other hand a realism which embraces the unbroken power of Eros, and at the same time accepts the laws of sociology and politics.

It is possible to express this Personalism—and Buber has more than once done so—in the conceptual framework of the Philosophy of Life: and in that case the heart of being, life and spirit is found in what Buber calls the 'I-Thou' relationship, while the surrounding world defined from that centre, and everything that is not included in the 'I-Thou' relationship, is correctly, though dangerously defined as the objective world of 'I-it'. This definition is not in itself bad, except in so far as it spreads and overlays the 'I-Thou' relationship, and because of its tendency to do so. But with the help of that conceptual framework, Buber can sum up the tragedy of Israel's history, and in a sense of all history, in one sentence: 'Once a culture is no longer centred upon a perennially renewed "I-Thou" relationship and the events which spring from it, then it petrifies into a world of "it" which the glowing actions of isolated spirits will only from time to time disturb as they erupt through the crust.' (24)

Chief Rabbi Löw, already mentioned (R. Loewe ben Bezalel), lays down the following principle in his theological history of Israel: 'Every creature exists in the relative perfection of its specific kind; only the creature whose kind approaches perfection is imperfect in his own kind. And so it is with Israel, whose children are more definitely the children of God than those of any other nation: but that high characteristic did not ripen to perfection in them. As imperfect of their perfect kind, they stand below the Angels; but their advantage consists in what they lack; as distinct from the angels, they can "become" . . . and because they are capable of becoming perfect, they are nearer to God than the angels.' (25) St Thomas more than once used the same principle, in a different context, and this offers a basis for discussion of the problem of natural and supernatural as it affects Israel. On the one hand, St Thomas says that the highest being of a lower order participates in the perfection of the order of being above him. But although that may be true, it does not help to solve the present question, because the natural and the supernatural are not related as though they were two kinds of being. On the other hand, St Thomas says that (as opposed to the animal creation) man's incapacity to perfect himself in his own purely natural order, and the fact that he is orientated towards divine grace, result in his imperfection itself being the sign of his particular and special worth and level of being. (26)

That proposition goes to the heart of the tension between natural and supernatural, within which, as it were, man's being is actually situated: since the man who understands himself in the light of the Bible can only understand himself as created for the order of grace, for the dialogue with God, and because, on the other hand, however his natural end may finally be conceived, he can never lay claim to access to the intimate sphere of the divine. Otherwise grace would not be grace. It is difficult to continue in that state of tension; philosophical personalism almost always succumbs to the danger of making a sort of necessity of the ultimate freedom of the divine revelation, which corresponds to the laws applying to the creation. And yet Buber is unquestionably right, not only as concerns his own position, but where the Christian is concerned, when he affirms that the separation or bracketing-off which revelation itself imposes, must not be glossed over in favour of a sort of inverted philosophical necessity, and in such a way that the factual definition of man appears to be replaceable, hypothetically, by others. The consequence of this is—and this is equally true from the Christian point of view—an unbreakable bond between philosophy and theology, or between a philosophical and a theological anthropology and cosmology, unbreakable because both points of view have and only can have a single object: the one natural and supernatural world with its dual aspect of creation and covenant. So that it is not at this point that there is any opposition between Jewish and Christian thought. The personalism of Ferdinand Ebner and of Gabriel Marcel are evidence of this.

The discordance between the Jewish and the Christian points of view breaks out at another point where Israel, mishandling its own history, forcibly resolves the tension between natural and supernatural by identifying the two—with the result that it comes to regard its earthly task as coinciding with the Kingdom of God. This is done in the name of the sacramental principle, which is a prolongation, as we have seen, of the prophetic principle. The order of God coincides with the true social order, which extends from the ethical sphere to the political. Pursuing its 'impossible' Utopian task, Israel reaffirms the identity of natural and supernatural at a deeper level, and prompted by an irrepressible instinct that it will one day give birth to the absolute as the very fruit of its body. 'The messianic idea is the profoundest and the most original idea of Judaism. It is well to ponder what it means: the Jew has undertaken to build a house for mankind, the hearth of the true life, in the future—in that eternally distant but eternally near sphere which like the horizon retreats before us but never gets farther away—in the kingdom of the future where only changing, unstable and lambent dreams can penetrate . . . It was bound to happen, every moment testified to it; there was warrant for it in the blood, and God himself sanctioned it. . . That which was to come was often something altogether relative, the liberation of a tortured people, reunited round their sanctuary, but at its supreme moment, at the high point, it was the absolute, mankind's salvation and the salvation of the world. . . . There, for the first time, we see the absolute proclaimed with power and authority, as the *end* to be realised in and through mankind.' (27)

But what in fact is that 'eternally distant, that infinitely near'? What exactly does future mean if it is both temporal and absolute, which means to say breaking through time? The sacramental existence of Israel in the Holy Land requires that there should also be a 'holy time' corresponding to the holy place: the human form of duration, with the future in view must, where Israel is concerned, acquire the meaning of salvation. But how is it possible for the 'eternal' to break out from this conception of time if not as the result of a qualitative change, a leap—unless, that is, one discovers the eternal through that 'instant', and transposes it into the absolute impulse towards the future which fills Israel and constitutes its soul. 'In Judaism, the decisive event is happening all the time, which is to say it happens here and now. Even the horizon of the "last things" pales before the ripe fullness of destiny in the here and now. Projected forward in time, the Kingdom of God appears upon the face of the absolute future, where heaven and earth touch one another; timeless in the present, it reveals itself ever and again in the instant, where the union of God and his destiny (*Schechina*) occurs in the real acts of the true man.' (28) 'The image of a perfect *time* is projected "in the form of a messianic eschatology", and the image of 'a perfect *place* in the form of a Utopia'. And in spite of the fact that the two conceptions conflict, they are nevertheless held together because while 'presenting perfection in the light of the absolute, they present it as something towards which there is an active path leading out of the present. Thus what appears impossible as a concept arouses, in the form of an *image*, the power of faith, and so determines the design and the plan.' (29)

And in fact the Prophets had always created images: the image of Israel returning home from exile and banishment and focusing the nations, their powers, and their gifts, in the light of its Holy of Holies: Jerusalem becomes the soul of the world and of its history. Yet Buber's regressive tendency, his urge to turn back to the source and his refusal to recognise the direction of Jewish history as a genuine and necessary development (the Kingdom, the Exile and finally the post-exile period broadening out in the direction of Christianity), becomes in this instance a tendency to be satisfied with a philosophical 'eternity in the instant of time'. 'That which is to come' is existentially speaking that which is. And so the Christian dimension of death and resurrection drops out or is left out because it distracts attention from the earthly task in which the individual man and mankind are immersed. What is demanded of the people is that they should exist before JHWH, that their heart be converted and their whole activity orientated towards 'the day of the Lord'. If the true model of socialism is to be held up to mankind, then the inward, ethical aspect and the external, political aspect must coincide, the heart must be in the deed.

In *Paths in Utopia* Buber put his finger unerringly on the point where Marx evaded the real issue, the problem of integrating the inward, ethical aspect of socialism, and pin-points the moment when Marx sacrificed it in favour of a purely external, political solution out of which the ethical aspect is then supposed to erupt automatically and as though by magic in the dialectic of history and give us the age of freedom. When Vera Zasulitsch put the operative question to him (30) and asked how the Russian village was to be transformed in view of the coming revolution: whether it was to be organised organically or politically (which meant that the 'archaic forms' were to be allowed to disappear and would be thought out and planned anew by a town-dwelling proletariat), Marx hesitated and gave an ambivalent answer. The fact that he wrestled with the question shows that he was fully alive to the ultimate consequences of his decision. The solution which he gave, and which was meant to reconcile the two aspects, was in fact self-contradictory: factually, historically, the political element dominated. (31) And that meant that the role of the individual, personal freedom and a genuine personal faith were discarded.

Now this is the point where the final problems of post-Christian Jewish eschatology emerge. In Marx's system, the personal, 'inward' act, in a word conversion, is overlaid, suppressed or repressed by the political element. But the classical period of Israel, down to the period of the Babylonian exile, did not allow of an individual eschatology. The believer's duty was to embody his own personal act of faith, so that it became part of the obedience of 'the people' moving towards a messianic future—and that had to suffice him for this world and the next. But if he is to remain consistent, Buber must also reject any form of development in the individual's view of the future life, judgment, purification and resurrection, as being unbiblical, a decadent, apocalyptic and, from a religious point of view, a highly questionable development. He is driven to make man rest content with the notion of a temporal, sacramental setting for his existence, with its eternal perspectives and its surrender to God, but to deny him even so much as a questioning gaze beyond the grave. It is better for him to scan the temporal future, where he will discover the urgent tasks of the people in which it is his duty to take part.

Buber is therefore driven more and more—against his will —into the ethos of socialism as presented by contemporary Marxism. But the question arises whether his refusal to read the history of Israel in the direction in which it flows, and his attempt to relate the primitive sources of Judaism to the present time, while overleaping all the intermediate Jewish and Christian elements (as though the man of today could hope to suppress Job's question, or those which the Psalmist asks about man's eternal destiny), does not in fact lead Buber into an entirely unintentional and avoidable dualism, which is no longer clearly thought out, and that comes to light in his anthropology—where we find two quite distinct images of man confronting one another. There we find a social and collective conception of man derived from a harmless optimism and perfectionism; and a conception of man derived from the prophet standing in the midst of that earthly paradise so busily organised by the collective: a tragic, tortured figure who can ultimately only be condemned to death and crucified. Whatever may be said or done, the two cannot be reconciled. Both Judaism and Christianity are agreed that at this point it is necessary to choose between a general philosophical, cosmopolitan wisdom, a sort of Wisdom for Everyman that will satisfy everyone, and the real prophecy of Israel that was always surrounded by a sense of scandal and was conscious of being humbled.

CHAPTER FIVE

Israel and the Nations

IT CAN now be seen that the ultimate question propounded by the Prophetic and the Sacramental principles, though left open, and apparently unalterable and without issue, nevertheless leads back to the central mystery of Israel's existence. Martin Buber's struggle to hold the extremes of his position together, and not to sacrifice either, is not simply a move in the dialectical game but the struggle upon the outcome of which his very existence depends. Israel is a nation like other nations and races, but with this difference: it is not governed by racial laws and customs, nor by the force of destiny, but by God himself because he chose it for the sake of the others. (1) And it is precisely for that reason, because of its universal mission which sets it apart from other nations, that Israel must be a specific nation like others—not just a 'spiritual kingdom' like the Christian Church—it must be related to that universal mission in a purely individual and characteristic manner. That is why the Jewish nature can only be properly described in terms of a theology (of election) which is always open to a universally valid philosophical anthropology.

Buber's earliest attempt to supply that theology and the implied anthropology began with the second factor or pole, with the relation between the specifically Jewish nature and the universally human. He maintains that what is specifically

Jewish is at the same time the most fully articulate expression of the universally human—and not 'a particular qualitative definition' of the human; indeed it would be truer to reverse the statement and to say that the universally human element stands out more strongly, more purely in Judaism than elsewhere. (2) The dualism which is so characteristic of Jewish thought and of the Jewish mentality, is more articulate, more radical than in any other culture, and so too, consequently, is the impulse to achieve unity, not only in God but in the world, and furthermore between God and the world. Their feeling for unity is not only deeper, more urgent, but provides the example and model for others. (3) That dualism or discord which we see in all the great biblical figures (4) as well as in modern Judaism with its 'unbelievably tragic depths' (5) is the driving force that impels Israel to seek for the unity and salvation of all. Judaism is in fact the basic form of humanism, though the word is no longer used in the same sense as that of the Jewish humanists (6) nor in the platonic sense of humanism as an idea or ideal, but as something very real, the driving-wheel of history, perceptible or imperceptible. Moreover, Israel is justified in making this great claim to be exemplary in this respect because, as we have already seen, it links sacred and profane, confidence in God to confidence in the land, in a way no other people has been able to emulate or rival because it is Israel's supernatural mission.

It is characteristic of this supernatural task that it is not historically imposed from heaven. On the contrary, despite the uniqueness and the exceptional character of Israel's religion, it forms part of the religious history of the human race out of which it emerges, and therefore remains in touch with it both in its positive and its negative aspects. For what man says about God is always expressed in images and myths;

'all living forms of monotheism are full of the mythical element, and they only remain alive as long as that remains the case. It is true that the rabbinical élite, in its blind determination to circumscribe Judaism, attempted to formulate a faith in God "purified" of its mythical element, though all it succeeded in producing was "a miserable homunculus".' (7) In the final canon of Holy Scripture, the priesthood did its utmost to exclude 'everything mythical from the full text of the scriptures as they had been handed down. . . Fortunately their imperfect knowledge prevented them from achieving their aim, and a good deal of the material, the original character of which they no longer understood, escaped their notice.' (8) That is why (in spite of the bowdlerisation) it is still possible to see in the Bible how the particular is formed of universal elements and expresses itself in them and then, deepened by immersion in Israel, those universal elements are made available to mankind as a whole. In Israel, the universal receives a 'special significance' (9); it is crystallised, or is realised in a religious form which is found paralleled among other early peoples, but never with the same concrete historical character. (10) As we know from experience, the consciousness of being chosen, of having a special mission, is part of the universal religious element; and so is the claim to be a model. But if one follows out these ideas consistently, it becomes difficult to describe the special character of Israel except in terms of intensity, as a heightening of what is already present, and then there is a real danger that the theological aspect will be reduced to a dialogical principle, itself part of a philosophy of religion.

Buber has undoubtedly felt the danger, and in the course of his long life he has more than once turned back to the problem of giving his thought a solid theological foundation and a clear formulation, regardless of the consequences. In the first phase of his work the emphasis is on the kinship of Israel with everything human—that was in the years before the First World War, and the same viewpoint reappeared during the optimistic period between the 1914 war and the advent of the Nazis. Later the emphasis falls more and more on the singularity and isolation of Israel in the world. 'The fact of Israel's existence,' he writes, 'is unique, and cannot be fitted in anywhere. The very name, not inherited from father and mother, but given by God to the father of the race, marks out the community as a community which cannot be apprehended in the categories of ethnology or sociology.' (11) 'Zion,' he writes again, 'is not simply an exceptional instance of the national idea, or a national movement; the particular thing which is superadded in this case to the universal creates a separate genus so far above and beyond the frontier of the national problems that it touches on the frontier of human and cosmological problems, and on the problem of being itself.' (12)

Moreover Zionism demonstrates that 'those who have embarked upon this colonising undertaking are a people and what is more a people who are virtually indefinable, indeed a *problematical* people: in the first place it is stateless, without the protection afforded by the State; secondly it is landless, without the cohesion communicated by a particular place or site; and thirdly it possesses no bond to hold it together, neither a unifying order nor any form of leadership. That is where the paradox of Zion is new and unique. There has never been anything like it in the history of the world, and it contradicts the "laws" of politics.' (13) Israel is a people and Palestine is a country like any other, but the bond that links them together is a mystery. That bond confers a perfectly authentic right on Israel, although it cannot be adequately formulated in terms of the *droit des gens*. And indeed the peoples who helped Israel to obtain its rights certainly felt something of the mystery even though they could only express themselves in humanitarian and legal language.

How liberating those words of Buber's are, and how decisive too! No doubt the choice which led up to that affirmation could be traced back to the very earliest years when Buber rejected a purely political Zionism in favour of a divinely instituted, sacramental bond between people and land. But in fact the choice is so absolute and unyielding, so exclusive, that Israel is forced into the position of being utterly isolated from the nations of the world, so that the bond between people and land is hardly relevant to the majority of Jews in the new Israel, and Buber himself remains apart in their midst. But the new Jerusalem cannot arise in the Argentine or Uganda, and Palestine is not a choice dictated simply by piety—Zion and Zion alone is Israel's home. And at that point the relativism of a philosophical religion ceases to apply; in its place we find a rock-like foundation, we get down to dogma. Dogma is always recognisable from the fact that it is a stone of offence; its intransigence is a scandal to the tolerant who can reduce any system of religious concepts to any other system. The dogmatic character of the affirmation is apparent from the scandal aroused by the unconditional bond linking an impossible prophetic mission to an earthly, sacramental sign: the land.

It can certainly do no harm and might be a good thing to interpret and live that bond as spiritually as possible. What is at stake is Abraham's election to 'a prophetic existence', which is 'as old as Israel'. (14) At this point it does not matter how much Buber talks about the 'two forms of faith' which he regards as irreconcilably opposed. The fact remains that Judaism, as he understands it, and Christianity, as the Catholic Church interprets and represents it, are the last two witnesses to an absolute mission in the world, given by God—absolute in the 'scandalous' sense of an obligation binding man to the particular and visible, 'thus and thus only'. For everything else can be melted down and made interchangeable in terms of anthropology, sociology and psychology, and by a series of permutations reduced to a 'philosophical faith'. Buddhism, Tao, Gathas, Sumeria and Egypt, Hellenic wisdom and the ecstatic religions of all peoples, which Buber values and loves, each have their own root, but all debouch in the end into the universally human. One can enter into their spiritual treasure-house, choose and assimilate what one likes, because it is part of the universally human. The outer envelope can be discarded as dated, and the nourishing kernel retained. But there are two religious structures in the religious history of the world which cannot be acquired on those terms: no one who is not a Jew can become one; and those who have become Christians through baptism cannot cease to be Christians. Jew and Catholic may only have exchanged a few words in more than a thousand years and have turned their backs on one another; they may remain indifferent to one another, or even inimical: but they are nevertheless indissolubly bound together, tied back to back throughout the ages to form a sort of whipping-post or pillory—for 'the people of God', old and new, together, is a single, indivisible scandal. As for the rest, they can always find a diplomatic way out; they can use the humanist's freedom and 'the freedom of the Christian': Israel and the Church know no way out.

Buber himself has admitted that this may well be the point where Jew and Christian might begin their lonely dialogue. 'Israel is unique . . . and cannot be fitted into any genus or category. There is no pigeon-hole in history made to take Israel. . . . That is the one position from which we Jews can speak to the Christians, for that is the only situation which offers the existential possibility of an answer. . . . Only we two, the Church and Israel, know what Israel really means.' (15) But it is a dialogue that takes place within a contradiction as it were, 'and where the disagreement is harsher than any merely logical contradiction. For the Church looks upon Israel as *rejected* by God. That rejection necessarily follows from the Church's claim to be the real Israel.' (16)

It therefore becomes necessary to consider what rejection means in the New Covenant. The principal text, which Buber never quotes, as far as I know, is Romans 9-11, where the hard and fast concepts of divine election and rejection are first minted, and then applied to the dialectic of the history of the Kingdom of God. The best commentary on the passage is certainly Karl Barth's solid and convincing elucidation (17), which no theologian can from now on afford to overlook. We can learn from him how to read the words of St Paul as he speaks in crystal-clear terms of the dialectic of election and rejection, and as Buber very well knows, what is more, he speaks of it as a matter which is in the first instance a Jewish one: the issue between Esau and Jacob (9, 13) that broadens out into the great issue of the mass of the lost and the 'remnant' who are saved in the theology of the Prophets (9, 27; 11, 5); and then going on from that point to the final historical form of the question, the relation between the Church and the Synagogue, though always preserving the typically Jewish structure or form with its 'alternatives'. St Paul makes use of that 'alternative' form with its threats and its promise, in the same eschatological way as Ezekiel (ch. 16), by expressing the dialectic of election and rejection in terms of the judgment and salvation of the world (18) in which, it is true, all men, Christian and Jew, are converted to faith but in which God's faithfulness to his choice is carried through: 'for the word of God has not miscarried' (9, 6). 'I say then; Hath God cast away his people? God forbid. . . God hath not cast away his people which he foreknew' (11, 1-2). 'I say then: Have they so stumbled that they should fall? God forbid. . . Now if the fall of them be the rising of the world, and the diminishing of them the riches of the Gentiles; how much more their fullness?' (11, 11-12) 'The blindness in part has happened in Israel, until the fullness of the Gentiles should come in; and so all Israel should be saved' (11, 25-26). 'For the gifts and the calling of God are without repentance' (11, 29).

No Jew who knows the Scriptures would deny that the words which St Paul uses in his argument are borrowed from the Old Testament treasury of thoughts and words and left unaltered. What here befalls Israel has often befallen her before, and indeed more clearly and more tragically. It is in fact the same 'alternative' that Buber has so often developed with so much feeling, the blending of light and dark, the same chiaroscuro which he shows us in Jeremiah and Job, and the deutero-Isaiah. And so if Buber reproaches the Church with regarding Israel as rejected and behaving to it as such, then he can only be taking the word in its ordinary, rough and ready, vulgar sense, in which case he is more or less right as far as Christendom is concerned. But if the theological and dialectical sense is intended (and dialectical here includes what Buber calls dialogical), the meaning does not depend in any way upon human opinion, as though a conciliatory attitude on the part of Christians could be of any help in toning down or mitigating the sense, any more than the Jewish enlightenment or historical theology could minimise the severity of the prophets.

Yet it would be a mistake to magnify the paradox of this discussion by denying or failing to make it clear that the two parties involved, though they may only speak to themselves, are in reality implicated in a dialogue. Buber would like to make out that this is only true of one of the partners in the dialogue, namely the Christian, and that it does not apply to the Jew. The truth you possess, he says to the Christian in effect, you owe to us, and you are obliged to steep yourself again and again in it if you want to be cured of your Greek or Manichean or even Pauline habits of thought. Wherever Christianity is cut off from its Jewish roots, it goes astray from a Christian point of view, for the foundation stock of the synoptic gospel of Jesus is in fact a purely Jewish stock, whereas the Johannine and Pauline variations on the synoptic themes reveal definitely gnostic characteristics, at least as regards certain basic motifs—whether one likes to call gnosticism Greek or late Jewish. But the Church has been careful not to deny this part of the truth: if Jesus Christ is to be regarded as a true man and as the fullness of time, as the culminating point in the history of salvation, and if he is to be understood by mankind in general, then he must unquestionably be seen in the context of a continuous historical time and of an historical salvation. For nothing historical falls from heaven—more particularly when it is a unique event, a vertical factor, so to say, its credibility and the testimony to its truth derives from its horizontal position in the temporal succession of events which are known to us as the prophetic relation of the promise to the fulfilment, which Jeremiah himself uses as a testimony to the truth. Starting from that point, and moving on the spiritual path of that which is to come, man can find access to the presence of the absolute Word in history. 'The woman saith to him: I know that the Messias cometh (who is called Christ); therefore, when he is come, he will tell us all things. Jesus saith to her: I am he, who am speaking with thee' (Jn. 4, 25-26). That is not only true in the sense that the man Jesus was born of a Jewish woman, but in the far wider sense that the one incarnate Word comes to us from the many words in which God 'spoke in times past to the fathers by the prophets' (Heb. 1). That does not mean to say that he comes to us as a river, quantitatively enriched from many sources, so that those who know the confluents have only to recognise the final syncretism in the river itself, and could indeed calculate its character, but in the manner in which the Word of God always came in times past to the fathers: prophetically, as something altogether incalculable, coming down from above, sovereign and free.

But at this point Buber refuses to admit the reverse of his truth. No doubt he recognises all the individual elements in the Jewish position: he allows, in the first place, that a Jew reflecting upon Judaism will discover the future elements of Christianity in it; he equally allows that there is a movement towards what is Christian within Judaism itself; and finally that the specifically Christian element is a new deposit which cannot simply be regarded as derived from the Jewish element, and that the Jew therefore, seeing what is new does not receive it as his own, but feels it as something foreign. But to Buber these various factors do not link up to form the historical structure of truth whose two poles are the promise and the fulfilment. His view of the Jewish conception of prophecy is wanting in the transcendent element implied by fulfilment; it never rises above itself, and because it remains imprisoned within the scheme of its own thought, it is finally precipitated into the paradox already mentioned of social Utopianism. And as a result the new Christian element can only be viewed as something foreign, and not as the fulfilment, despite the fact that everything within Judaism is prepared for that new perspective. It is of course prepared in the main by the current of history which brings the advent of salvation step by step nearer, in the form of the Son of God, a saviour who dies and rises again. But it is precisely that movement, that direction, which Buber insists upon interpreting rigidly and consistently as a purely immanent movement, in Spenglerian terms, so to say, as a gradual degeneration. And this interpretation obliges him to work in the opposite direction, to think against the stream, always going back to the Jewish source. Where Buber is concerned, therefore, the principle of Judaism is unquestionably the prophetic principle, but it is not prophecy pointing towards fulfilment in Christ: on the contrary, it is prophecy resting in itself yet filled with a profound unrest.

Before going any further, we shall do well to admire the sheer audacity of his affirmation. Cut off by its uniqueness from the religions of peoples which can be wholly expressed in philosophical and universal terms, Israel is cut off too from its sister people, the Christians, by its refusal to allow the prophetic principle its transcendent culmination in a fulfilment given by God alone, and then again by its refusal to look for the solidarity of love in the one Jewish-Christian salvation. Israel is therefore immobilised and cruelly isolated, and that isolation inevitably infects the Church to a certain extent. That isolation is the first and fundamental Schism (19) which robs the Church of the unity intended by providence, causing the rift between the Old and the New Covenant. And it is for that reason, the failure of Judaism to respond, that the Church fails to recognise itself fully in the Old Testament, and in consequence is obliged to content itself with 'texts' when really it needs the living heart of Judaism. The Church cannot permanently be satisfied with anything short of the heart of Israel. It does not want its praise of God to derive simply and solely from the written word, but from the mind and heart of the Jews at prayer, from those who first formed the words, so that it can embrace them in its living tradition. (20) The Church recognises that the structure and dimensions of her life and growth are those of Judaism, and it could never think of treating the pagan traditions as though they were of the same dignity as the Jewish tradition for the simple reason that the Church is constituted of 'Jew and Gentile'.

Israel's innermost nature implies a Christology, and if it ponders on its own nature it should be able to recognise within itself the Christianity with which it is pregnant. But it is that process of 'becoming' that is all important; and it is time to consider in what sense the promise informs the whole conception of Israel and how far it could become conscious of its own nature. That we are saying little that is new will be obvious to anyone who is at all familiar with the fundamentals of Christian theology: from the Fathers down to the present day, the same things have been said over and over again. But there is no point in just brushing them up a little and displaying them as before to an original thinker like Buber; they need to be thought out anew and formulated in the light of a full and virile notion of revelation.

The older theologians are doubtless right when they say that Israel is the visible, earthly, and fleshly sign or parallel of what was to be fulfilled spiritually in Christianity. It is, moreover, self-evident that 'spiritual' does not mean incorporeal, since the fulfilment consists in the incarnation of the Word. But for the moment that is not the point; what we have to consider more closely is the fact that Israel's prophetic and sacramental principles are ultimately defined by the promise.

It becomes evident in the light of that characteristic—and the promise implies that Israel is also the forerunner—that there is an irreducible contradiction at the very heart of Israel. Nothing brings that out so clearly, or indeed so painfully, as the way in which Martin Buber presents it. Israel is the chosen among nations, chosen for the sake of others, but set apart in such a way that there is no access to it: no one can become a Jew. Proselytising is simply impossible. The source of the community of nations is itself incommunicable —to such an extent is this true that not even the children of mixed Jewish and non-Jewish marriages may be looked upon as a sort of 'synthesis'. That is the ultimate contradiction latent in the Jewish task, and it is made still more evident by the two-fold existence of the Jews: for they are dispersed among the nations—yet reunited in their own country (assuming that the attempt is successful in the long run). But as long as Israel is dispersed—and Israel sometimes looks rather timidly upon the dispersal as an occasion for working among the Gentiles (21)—Israel is not truly itself, and really interprets its condition as the punishment of God. Banished from the Land, it grows sick and cannot heal itself. (22) It is of course possible for Israel to be recalled from exile and reunited—and that is one of the great messianic promises common to all its historical phases. But in that case it ceases to be the leaven of the world in a geographical sense; it is turned in upon itself and loses touch with the outer world, and in the eyes of Israel the Gentiles who remain within its territories are there as a punishment from God (Judges 1, 27; 2, 5). When it is free to move about the world, as well as free in a spiritual sense, Israel has no centre from which to draw consistency as a nation; and the moment it is reunited, it can only be an example through its isolation. What it lacks in fact is the possibility of an apostolate, because the very concept of an apostle, the notion of someone sent out to proselytise, does not tally with Judaism. One might almost say that Israel's life, the movement of its life, is an eternal return from the dispersion. The movement of the Church is the exact opposite, a centripetal movement, going out to all the nations of the earth at all times: and in fulfilling that movement it is not dispersed or exiled, but in its very element, its proper situation. What the Jews can never hope to unite is identical in the Christian context: home and abroad—an idea so movingly expressed in the Epistle of Diognetes:

'For the Christians are not distinguished from other men by the countries in which they live, the language which they speak, nor by their customs; they live in any town, they use any language and do not lead a life which calls attention to them. . . . They live in Greek towns and towns that are not Greek according as destiny ordains in each particular instance . . . though they are only there as visitors. They take part in everything as though they were citizens, and accept everything as though they were strangers. Wherever they happen to be is their fatherland, and whatever fatherland it happens to be is a foreign country to them.' (25)

Perhaps it is becoming clear now why the young Hegel was

destined to discover the framework of his philosophical dialectic in the theological relation between the Old and the New Covenant. His understanding of Christ's synthesis required a clear grasp of the thesis and antithesis of Israel. Hegel, it is true, interpreted them as 'tragic' and 'conflicting', and allowed far too little weight to the positive pedagogical element, the preparation for the coming of Christ. For in this case, as in others, the antithesis and the historical contradiction would not exist if the synthesis did not lie hidden behind them; for the Law and the Prophets are there for the sake of Christ, and were ordained for his sake, and consequently they are only fully intelligible as the promise, and seen after Christ. The origin and end of all forms of dialectic can indeed be discovered in the dialogue between the Old and the New Covenant—in the dialogue which neither the Old nor the New Covenant like to remark upon, but in which light and salvation are always to be found.

The question which Israel raises is indeed so radical that it can only be answered absolutely. The answer cannot be found on the level on which Israel, given its assumptions, would naturally like to suggest. But the answer must nevertheless unite the two factors which cannot be united in the question: those and none other. That certainly calls for a 'reduction', though not in Buber's sense. The answer, as one says in mathematics, will have to 'reduce' both Land and Temple (with its priesthood, its sacrifice, its customs) to the body, the 'flesh', of the Word of God, which in the living man, Jesus Christ, becomes the unifying principle. Furthermore Christ is not only a unifying principle in that he is a man, alive and free (as opposed to purely material things, Land and Temple), but in a far wider sense, in that he dies and rises again through the strength of God; the whole situation or relationship is thus raised to a new level and given a further dimension, so that his death and resurrection acquire a new sense: that of judgment upon sin and salvation from it. That is the only possible release from the contradiction between Land and Exile, and release, at the same time, from the pure spirituality of the prophetic principle and the absolute bond of the material, geographical element in the sacramental principle of Land and Temple. The dispersed are indeed reunited, but the reunion is now eucharistic, reunion in the body of Christ which is the Church—and that, moreover, is the one sense in which the Didache includes the Jewish prayer for reunification in the new liturgy. (26) For it is after the Eucharistic communion that the dispersal throughout the nations of the earth begins again: *Ite, missa est*. The Church certainly owes that experience, which the Christians felt as a great marvel and a great gift of grace (27), to Christ, but the Church also owed it to his and its Judaic origins—not to some borrowed stoic or possibly hellenistic cosmopolitanism. The new Temple and the new Sacrifice, however, are enduring: they do not have to be set aside as superannuated and superfluous, as happens in Buber's 'prophetic reduction'; they are taken up into the 'temple of his body' and in 'the sacrifice of himself': there is no breach in the continuity; everything is progressively fulfilled and leads into unity and not, as Buber would have it, as the result of a disintegrating regression towards some ideal origin. That progress towards Christ implies, before all else, the opening of heaven, in a sense which becomes more and more vividly proclaimed in Jewish history until the moment when the word of God became flesh in Christ and God himself became historical. But Buber will not allow the beyond to be incorporated in the present, here and now; he prefers to close the doors on eschatology—in the belief that once the debauch begins there is no stopping it.

Nevertheless, even when circumscribed in terms of this world, Israel can still always imply the absolute; and what it is undertaking at the present time, and all that it can ever attempt in that direction, is the best counter-proof of what has already been said about its role as the precursor. Thesis and antithesis are pincers whose two arms are made to grasp the absolute. When they do not hold the synthesis of the Word of God and Man, of obedience and freedom, they are left empty-handed and open for ever, with no object conforming to their purpose. The dynamism that should have the eternal for its goal hurls itself instead upon the future in time, thus missing and betraying one of the essential features of Judaism: the tragic and prophetic situation which prefigures the Christian idea of 'mortification', that is, of dying with Christ. And then that self-same dynamism is in grave danger of becoming anti-Christian and demoniacal, of assuming one of the forms of absolutism that lay waste the world, such as capitalism in the West and Communism in the East. Man is looked upon as good and able to save himself; he has the power to convert not only himself but the whole world, transforming the community and changing the face of the earth in order to make them, too, good. Man is on the path to Utopia which Buber would like to make into a path that leads towards a sacred and prophetic idea; but in the Israel of today those paths lead to an almost wholly secular world where there is precious little religion! Between *The Socialism of the Future* where the tragic note is absent, and the personalism to which Buber has now turned, and where that note is present, there is a wide gulf—a sign of Israel's mission as precursor.

But the Jew may well counter what has been said with a

question: Have you Christians a genuine relation to the realities of this world? What do the State, work and the future of mankind matter to you? Of course there is a place for them all in your works of apologetics, and you fit them in politely and tidily: you defend the natural law, but for all that it remains strangely unreal because you cannot throw yourselves honestly into the affairs of this world. You overleap these spheres with the help of a single idea, the salvation of the world. Whether there is more justice and sin in the world or less does not seriously disturb you. Your Christ, who conquered the world, did not commission you to nourish and shape our worldly world. You are content to wait for the end and see no reason to put your hand to the plough. You are justified by faith, and if you defend works then it is simply for the sake of heaping up treasure in the eternal barns. Your treasure is in heaven, and so that is where your heart is. You are and remain dualists, and your interest in the future of the world, which you have somewhat tardily begun to proclaim after two thousand years of Christianity, is no more than an 'as if', a pretty transparent hypothesis not quite honestly put forward. The *civitas terrena* is 'either the Kingdom of the eternally damned, as it was for Augustine, a world from which the elect must therefore dissociate themselves at once, or it is a merely preliminary stage, a school if you like for the true community that is to come (the Church), which is how it is regarded in Thomism.' (28) Israel, on the contrary, is a real state, blood and soil, *civitas dei et terrena* simultaneously, and as such it is delimited in the same way that the man Jesus was delimited, by time and space and mission: for what is incarnate cannot be spirit, that is, uncircumscribed. But the spiritual people which you Christians claim to be, has no earthly consistency, not even that of Jesus, whom St Paul 'no longer knows according to the flesh'. But since in this material world the spiritual cannot exist incorporeally, you have been obliged to fall back upon a state which even we Jews have long since abandoned, the rule of the priests; though their power is no longer held in check, as in our history, by a divinely safeguarded prophetic tradition; and once the prophet of tradition has been discarded the priestly power remains alone on the field, a monstrous anachronism. It is our turn, now, to point out your inner contradictions, the equivalent of and the parallel to the contradictions you thought you could discover in us; you go on talking about incarnation, but your God-man has simply distracted your attention from the human condition, and you continue to gaze into the clouds, like the men of Galilee as the Lord was hidden from their sight. You talk about the leaven, about a spiritual people, and you ramble on about freedom, but you, with your Church, have nothing to offer the nations and peoples of the world—nothing but your missions and the directives of your pastoral letters—while your freedom is only obedience to the clergy. And who is going to be tempted or attracted by that?

Surely there is a ready Christian answer to all this? Though perhaps it would be better to pause; a moment's silence and a little reflection might be all to the good, with the discussion resumed when both peoples have had time to think things over.

It is not the fault of Israel alone but of our common guilt and the stiff-necked obstinacy of the sinner which daily prevents the Church from appearing as Jesus wished it to be. If the Church were holy in its members, in us (and wherever that is the case one can perceive something of its nature), then it could be fruitful, and the leaven would be in the world and not merely alongside it. If it were altogether holy in its members there would be no gulf between office and charisma, priesthood and prophetic office, obedience to the body of Christ visible and obedience to the Holy Spirit in the Church. Peter must have the greatest love possible and follow Christ to the Cross (Jn. 21, 15-18). The unity is there from the beginning, in the plan, and it is only our sinfulness that prevents it from being realised. For that reason the unity of office and charisma can only be realised from time to time on the way of the Cross, and so become visible in that form to mankind. But at the same time one cannot say, with the Christian centuries in mind, that the community founded by Christ in the world has no history, or that its attitude has been purely and simply eschatological. Indeed, there never has been an idea or a reality which has polarised history so decisively and which has exacted and extracted so decisive a response as Christianity. It would be no less true to say that there is no ideal of any importance whatsoever which does not feel the influence of its star.

But there is one more step to take and we must have the courage to take it. If the Church does not stand out more convincingly and more persuasively it is certainly our fault. But it is also both our faults, and the people of the Old as well as the people of the New Covenant both share in the guilt. Buber is unquestionably right when he says that the Cross of Christ does not supervene like a dramatic end or catastrophe in a tragedy already foreseen, as though the drama which began at the crib and unfolded in the growing tension of Jesus's life had been unrolled like a film already taken. In spite of the prophetic figures and all the sayings that point towards the Cross, we must allow that God's messenger, coming from the Father to speak to his holy and

86

beloved people, knew a moment of unlimited and as it were paradisical simplicity and naïveté; for he desired to convert the People and make it follow him. He must therefore have thought that conversion was possible. For how could they resist and reject the Father's words? The offer of the Sermon on the Mount is an offer of severity and happiness in one; the heaviest burden becomes the lightest and easiest to bear once it is taken to heart and thus 'fully accepted'. But we can no longer hope to understand the turning point in Jesus's life, when he abandoned that first hope, because his loving attempts to win the people were only answered by the hardening of their hearts: the moment when he weeps over Zion. That is the moment when he can no longer carry out his mission except in suffering and by making a new beginning with his disciples, starting a 'schism' in fact within the Synagogue (a 'schism' which those who rejected him consummated), and only holding the new beginning together 'in his blood'.

That is the perspective in which the questions are addressed to Peter, and in which the rock and the keys must be understood. It is also in that perspective that one must ask to eat his body in order to live for ever. There is nothing in principle in the new priesthood and the new sacrifice which does not still correspond, even now, to what St Paul calls the spiritual and Buber the charismatic and which could not be expressed in our lives. Nevertheless, it is instituted in face of Israel's refusal, and Israel's guilt is reflected in it. And just as there is guilt at the very source, so is it administered in the midst of sinners, for them and by them, and it is they who give it the appearance which it has; and that in secret—and sometimes unrecognisably—is that of the Passion. An office in the Church, as its founder intended it, is all grace and light; but how can anyone not expect it to be misused? That is the heavy price that had to be paid for preserving the transcendental character of the Kingdom of God unbroken through the centuries: the unity of truth and the unity of love.

What people do not like about the Church, and what people do not like about the Synagogue, are the things which are our fault, our common fault. That alone is enough to show that the Church of Jesus cannot remain indifferent or adopt a purely objective attitude to Israel. The Church bears Israel and its earthly destiny along with her. The schism latent in Israel was brought to light by the judgment which is Christ and divides the New from the Old Covenant; it is neither more nor less than the fulfilment of the old prophetic judgment, which no one understands better than Israel. For the 'Greeks' always tended to misinterpret what it meant to stand under the judgment of God—but the Jews know what it means, and Buber has once again explained it.

So the question of Israel's mission comes again to the fore, more imperiously than ever.

CHAPTER SIX

Israel's Mission

THE ACTION of the New Testament is in the main concentrated at one point, in the breach: the abrupt dividing line between those who go farther and those who remain behind, between those who take the risk and make the leap, and those who shelter behind elaborate excuses and refuse. The sayings of Jesus are unmistakably judgments: they were repeated as such by the Apostles, and the first generations of Christians relied almost exclusively on those sayings. The inevitable is behind us, and there seems no sense in going back over it again. It all appears so simple to us in a worldly sort of way that we easily fail to notice that the judgment expressed in the word of God is delivered in the form of an alternative—a characteristic that reaches its final and culminating point in Jesus's words.

But the Jews knew of old how God always spoke to them. Jesus's words did not fall on untutored ears: Israel had learned to hear the alternative, to hear threat and promise in one, ever since Sinai and the end of Leviticus, since the meeting at Sichem, from Deuteronomy, Amos, Micah and Jeremiah, familiar with the proclamation of ever greater humiliations and harsher rejections linked to marvellous promises and demonstrations of divine faithfulness. As Buber points out, Jesus's words are in the great prophetic tradition and would be untrue to the core of that tradition if they did not express the alternative and did not have to be understood in that light. The segregation of the lost from the 'holy remnant' (1) was already an accomplished fact; the concepts and expressions of the 'New Covenant' were already coined so that what had become external might be anchored once and for all in the hearts of men. The prophecy of the destruction of the Temple repeats in a more intense form what had long since been announced and indeed accomplished. The rejection of Jesus was itself something wholly traditional, and astonishes no one: 'It cannot be that a prophet perish out of Jerusalem. Jerusalem, Jerusalem, that killest the prophets and stonest them that are sent to thee' (Lk. 13, 33-34).

But if the salvation of Israel is to be accomplished through the mediation of the 'remnant'—and ultimately through the servant of God who suffers for the guilt of all of us—and if the 'remnant' has become the new Israel of Jesus, then it is perfectly consistent with the logic of the divine word in Israel for the Old Covenant which remains behind to be judged by the 'remnant'. As Jesus himself says: 'You (the twelve representatives of Israel) shall sit on twelve seats judging the twelve tribes of Israel' (Mt. 19, 28: Lk. 22, 30), which is clearly one aspect of salvation: 'judgment should begin at the house of God' (1 Pet. 4, 17). If the 'remnant' may be called the 'form' of Israel's judgment, then Israel is the 'material' as far as the 'remnant' is concerned. And as Romans 11 explicitly says, that is what is intended, for it is the 'lump' which must be worked by the leaven.

Martin Buber asks that there should be some hope for Israel. It has never been refused him either in the Old or the New Covenant. It is hope through judgment; indeed as Israel has always known, the hope of judgment, hope in the day of the Lord. Between the hope and the fulfilment, however, there is a gulf: 'Israel hath not obtained that which he seeketh for; he seeketh for (epizêtei, the present), but the election hath obtained it, and the rest were blinded' (Rom. 11, 7). For the presence of salvation has moved away, and in its place there is a void: 'I have forsaken mine house, I have left mine heritage; I have given the dearly beloved of my soul into the hand of her enemies.' (Jer. 12, 7). 'The glory of the Lord departed from off the threshold of the Temple. . .' (Ez. 10, 18). 'Behold your house is left unto you desolate: and verily I say unto you, Ye shall not see me until . . .' (Lk. 13, 35.) But that teaching, as St. Paul explains, is the hour of salvation for the Gentiles who are streaming into the Kingdom of God, and since that was always the mission of Israel, it is also Israel's hour of salvation, and therefore its hope—but in the void. Everything said about those who are forsaken and about the glory which has departed from the Temple may be read as a consolation and as signifying a return: in Ezekiel it is even interpreted to mean not only a return to the Land and to the Temple built of stones, but the exchange of hearts made of stone for 'a new heart' and the gift of a 'new spirit' (Ez. 11, 19) and of new eyes with which to see those who have returned. 'And [verily] I say unto you, Ye shall not see me, until the time come when ye shall say: Blessed is he that cometh in the name of the Lord' (Lk. 13, 35; Ps. 108, 26).

Now those who newly enter the Kingdom do not sit down at a separate table, but explicitly at the same table as Abraham, Isaac and Jacob (Mt. 8, 11)—which forbids us from tearing the Old and the New Covenant apart, and once again recalls St Paul's image 'the holy tree' and the 'holy root' into which the wild branches will have been engrafted (Rom. 9; 11, 19). Israel must accept that engrafting and not grow envious of those who are not the people (Rom. 10, 19; Deut. 32, 21). It has got to stomach that final humiliation among all the humiliations heaped upon it, and endure the fact not only that its sisters, Samaria and Sodom, are justified before it (Ez. 16, 52ff), but that Israel will only be saved when 'the fullness of the Gentiles shall have come in' (Rom. 11, 25). Though what is called 'blindness' and 'obstinacy' and 'stiffness' is not a fate that befalls the individual; 'but even until this day when Moses is read, the veil is upon their heart; but, when they shall be converted to the Lord, the veil shall be taken away' (Ex. 34, 34; 2 Cor. 3, 15-16).

Peter's sense of solidarity with the Jews is such that he can address them in a way that is inconceivable and almost offensive to Christian ears: 'And now, brethren, I know that you did it through ignorance: as did also your rulers. But those things which God before had shewed by the mouth of all the prophets, that his Christ should suffer, he hath so fulfilled. Be penitent, therefore, and be converted, that your sins may be blotted out. That when the times of refreshment shall come from the presence of the Lord; and he shall send him who hath been preached unto you, Jesus Christ, whom heaven indeed must receive, until the times of the restitution of all things (Jer. 15, 19ff) which God has spoken by the mouth of his holy prophets, from the beginning of the world.' (Acts 3, 17-26).

The speech does not merely excuse the crucifixion and death of Jesus—Peter, who denied Jesus, knew how the risen Christ had behaved to him and he goes further; he sets the grace and the necessity of Christ's death, which had been announced so far back, so much above its unknowing instruments that it altogether outweighs their action. And so no opportunity is lost, conversion is possible at any moment, and the postponement of the Parousia nourishes the age-old expectation of Israel, justifying it anew and giving it an increased urgency: the conversion of all individual hearts will bring about the restitution, the apocatastasis which had always been promised. Peter does not lose this opportunity of touching on the old Jewish longing for the day of the Lord, although the risen Christ himself had turned the question put by his disciples about the time of the restitution of the Kingdom by referring to the mystery of the Father (Acts 7; cf. Mk. 13, 32), and directed the disciples instead to take up their universal mission. Peter defines the hour as being the coincidence of the will of the Father and the conversion of the human heart. Where Israel is concerned, the first and the second coming of Christ will therefore coincide, as may be seen from the beautiful play upon words: God allowed his servant to 'arise', which may refer either to the birth or the resurrection of the Lord and basically must imply both, because the coming of the second Adam as spiritual salvation is only consummated and fulfilled, as St Paul shows, in the resurrection (1 Cor. 15, 20ff; 45ff.). (2)

After as before, therefore, there is hope for Israel; and what is more, not hope in any ordinary sense, applicable to anyone, but its own special hope: the restitution and fulfilment of everything which *its* God, *its* prophets had always promised. But a hope which cannot be grasped, which exists in a void, it may be objected, cannot be a *task*; and that, after all, is what Israel is in search of. Can the question be discussed from a Christian point of view? It is a difficult one, and we can only hope to approach the answer slowly and come a little nearer to it.

One thing is certain, the continued existence of Israel, when considered in the light of that solidly and variously grounded hope, has a *meaning*. It lies, as always, in the un-breakable correspondence between promise and fulfilment with God. The fulfilment, is by definition at rest, while the former, the promise, is all movement (*Paid-agogia*), a dynamic notion that links a starting point to an end. It is at the beginning, when the promise is in a pure state, as it were, that the fulfilment is best seen across the centuries and all the historical phases of its realisation: for everything is rooted in the faith of Abraham. Though from another point of view it is furthest from the end and aim—historically the fulfilment is at first little more than a barely recognisable seed of grace sown among the pagan religious forms of the period, and only thrown into prominence much later by the sacred writers when it is set in a formal perspective and a liturgical language. (3) The history of Israel is the gradual permeation of a universal religious material by the leaven of its unique election, and this occurs in a succession of authentic phases leading up to the fulfilment. If the idea of development is applicable and useful in some form or other where the Church is concerned, it can only be in a secondary sense: the fullness once attained cannot, as such, develop—and while people talk somewhat loosely of the development of doctrine they really mean the reflective unfolding of depths of truth already present, the process by which we become conscious of them, which takes place in successive generations of Christians and as they are set forth by the teaching office of the Church; that process is naturally echoed in the prevailing conception of the Christian life, and in the response evoked by a deeper understanding. But in Israel progress and development in the basic sense of the words were implied and included in the revelation. The end to be reached presupposed something that had first of all to be understood, but that had either to be surpassed, spiritualised or even, in certain cases, discarded. Only the Old Testament can say Yea and Nay to the same thing at different times and depending upon the stage it has reached. The Temple of the Lord is untouchable, Isaiah says, when Jerusalem is threatened and with perfect justice: but later he will say that the Temple is not untouchable, and he will still be right. The just will be palpably rewarded in this life by God, thus hath God spoken, and his word has been proved in diverse ways—but when Job's friends presume to say the same thing, God adopts a different position: he takes a giant step forward and puts himself on Job's side.

The way in which God took Israel and educated it is un-exampled; in the course of a few centuries it leads from the ordinary human level, the sphere of the philosophy of religion, up through narrowing gorges, to the God-man. In a sense which is not exactly that which Buber wishes, the history of Israel is indeed a school, not only for Christians, but for man-kind as a whole, preparing them for the religion of Christ. It is the introduction ordained by God himself to the most intransigent of faiths, which falls like a meteor from heaven. Man must begin with his own thoughts on religion, with what is rather crudely called 'natural religion' and there is not a single idea, not a single thought in the religion of Israel—down to and including the most unique among them, such as the covenant, the kingdom, prophecy—which cannot be paralleled from a religious or sociological point of view; and, whether *a priori* or *a posteriori*, they can all of them be shown to be part of the universal religious phenomenon. But at the same time they always have a unique colour, and can be seen for what they are, God's signature in history. This is apparent from the fact that these unique thoughts are not simply or directly the product of Israel's 'religious genius'—on the contrary, Israel had always to be compelled, driven along in spite of its indolence, refractoriness and obstinacy, dragged along by the hairs of its head. And this allows us a glimpse of the dark recesses where the word of God has its source, of the depths where individual words and sayings each contribute to the powerful stream in which still impenetrable traditions are beginning to clarify: a dim and distant view of the birth and the becoming, when sayings and episodes, solitary or varied, are, as it were, transplanted so that they may flower and finally acquire their predestined meaning and their framework, which in retrospect often enough helps us to a deeper insight into the process by which they have come into being. That insight does not merely reveal the confusion and disorder of the inchoate. The clarity of the final result reflects the clarity of the origin which has directed the whole process: it implies an *a priori* in the field of revelation which no philological theory of the origins can undermine, and which becomes more distinctly clear theologically in the unity that has finally come about.

This conception of a dynamic tradition advancing from the level of world religions up to the absolute height and fullness of Christ—a conception close to that of the Old Testament, and clearly formulated by St Paul—cannot simply be reduced to, or explained away in terms of, that other conception according to which Israel is the fleshly parable of the subsequent spiritual reality. That second notional scheme was thrown into prominence by the platonising thought of the Epistle to the Hebrews, as it is called, and was then introduced by Alexandrian Christians into their systematic theology and their theology of history. Buber singles it out when he stresses the earthly character of Israel's mission and its 'this-worldly' character, so deeply opposed to the 'other-worldly' religion of Christ. Unfortunately the Alexandrian conception has proliferated within the Christian world until it almost threatens to choke the approaches to the New Covenant; and we are now at the stage of trying to clear the way. The ways which lead ever more clearly and definitely to Christ, are those which start from the beginning of the Exile and are not those of a degenerate apocalyptic belief, but of the original Judaic belief. They form the very core of Hosea's thought, and of Jeremiah's, and of the writings of the poet of the suffering servant. All of them are primarily historical and not literary ways, works which are the fruit of long suffering and not second-hand compilations. The transition which leads to Christ, historically speaking, is unique, but has always to be consummated anew; and the terrible sufferings in which the Messiah is born, seen by the visionary on Patmos in the image of the woman Zion-Maria, are never over. How can the fact that Israel suffers in secret or in exile be meaningless? How can something which is part of the history of salvation, and which was once an event —in the Old or the New Testament—ever lose its relevance and actuality, or cease being something in which we can participate? Moreover, that should not simply be understood in the sense of a moral example—as 1 Cor. 10, read superficially, might seem to insinuate—but in the sense that the word of God has sacramental power and is present at all times. But this cannot be stretched to mean that the biblical Fall is altogether indistinguishable from what is continually happening, as Buber seems to suggest. 'What happened once,' he writes, 'happens now and always, and the fact that it happens to us is a guarantee that it happened then. The Bible has given an eternally recurring event its decisive, expressive image in the form of a transforming recollection

... we owe (the) fundamental interpretation of our existence to the Hebrew Bible.' (4)

That is only one side of the truth; but because the other is wanting, and the original form of the unique historical revelation is disregarded, it looks as though mankind owed this interpretation to Jewish religiosity and not to the active word of God which has dealt with the Jews of those times and of today. And that would also mean that Israel, though its later history may run parallel to Christian history, remains permanently bound to the living sacramental character of its own period of revelation. In so far as it really remains the Israel of God, Israel can only be the people which waits in expectation, which is turned towards the Word in the Word of God. It is fully justified by the whole orientation and history of its revelation in not giving a literal interpretation to the historically primitive forms of its religion and cult, but in rejecting that 'fleshly' sense, as the sapiential literature (regarded by the Church as inspired) had already done, as did the Essenes, in favour of a spiritual interpretation. Moreover, the disagreements between Jesus and the scribes and Pharisees have a back history, the last phase of which we can glimpse in Qumrân.

It is certainly true that Israel's continued existence implies that it failed to attain the fulfilment, and this was expressed existentially during the great exile and the period of high expectation; and however eirenic the Christian approach to Israel may be, it cannot get round the fact. But it should at once be added that if the people of Israel feel the absence of the Church, then the Church, on its side, feels the loss of Israel; for, as the Fathers of the Church assure us, the scriptures of Israel rightly belong to the Church—but its books are not the whole living revelation: the heart of Israel is wanting. Whenever the unity of the people of God is broken by a schism, there is impoverishment; at the best that means that it must be judged and do penance. That is also true for the Church, and quite particularly of the primary schism, of which the earlier one between Judah and Israel and all the subsequent schisms within the Church are but reproductions. Certain aspects of Christ, and in this Buber is right, are only intelligible from within, to the Jew, and the faculty of understanding 'from within', that 'inside knowledge', ought by rights to be communicated to the Church from within. Not much can be done in this matter by books on the difference between the Greek and Hebrew ways of thought. The Church needs to absorb the understanding of salvation which is buried in Israel by digging down and striking root in the soil of its own pre-history. St Augustine saw this very clearly in the *Civitas Dei* and only lacked the necessary presuppositions, an authentic biblical theology, in order to be able to make his idea fruitful in every field. The weakest links in his work, as it stands, are the chapters on the history of Israel.

What providence intended was the unity of the two peoples, not the rift between them, the schism. Israel had it in its power to understand the spirit of its Messiah, and so to become the foundation stock of the people of God in that spirit—the spirit of poverty and humility, of the last place, of service to God and to the brethren, unto death and resurrection. How all this could have happened it would be idle to speculate. But it is by no means vain to reflect upon the fact that the divorce which uprooted the young Church from its mother-soil not only caused immeasurable harm to the Israel that remained behind, but involved a serious danger for the Church. Paul Démann is surely right when he puts his finger on the danger: 'The rift between the Church of the nations

99

and an isolated Israel resulted in the Church becoming to a certain extent *déraciné*. Very soon it found itself dangerously, though not of course entirely, cut off from its roots, estranged from the biblical fatherland of its forebears, and from an innate semitic way of thought, from the human soil in which the word of God was incarnate and in which, finally, the Logos himself became flesh. . . . The Church had therefore to become incarnate in other peoples and cultures, those of the hellenistic world . . . and that involved grave dangers. . . . This becomes obvious when it is a matter of translating the real living substance of the Church's message.' Démann holds that the first schism, between Jew and Christian, between the semitic and Asiatic elements on the one hand, and the hellenistic and western elements on the other, is at the source of all the subsequent great schisms in Christian unity, above all of course the schism between East and West. It was also at the source of the sixteenth-century schism, for Luther (with inadequate means) turned back to the semitic values and thought forms which had been lost or not fully-incorporated in the western tradition, and attempted to defend their rights as against a Greek and philosophical type of theology. No attempt to bridge the later breaches in the unity of the Church can be usefully pursued or seen in the light of a promising conclusion except with reference to the original schism from which they all follow. Nor is the matter between Israel and the Church one which can be studied as though it were a subsidiary oecumenical question; it needs to be treated in a quite different way, and far more radically than divisions among Christians. Above all, the problem of unity should not be formulated as though Israel were a people to be evangelised by missions of a rather special kind, and as though Israel were further from the Church than Christian sects. The sects are branches which have been separated and which should be re-engrafted—but Israel is 'the holy root' (Rom. 11, 16). And where St Paul's promise and explanation are concerned (the fact that the Gentiles are engrafted into Israel), it is pointless to regard Israel and the Church as two separate and distinct peoples of God, for there is only one people of God, only one *Civitas Dei*; and however true it may be that the Church is the new Israel, the final Israel and as the 'fullness of Christ' requiring no completion, nevertheless, on the historical plane, the development has not attained the final fullness foreseen as long as the angels have not 'gathered together his elect from the four winds, from the uttermost parts of the earth' (Mk. 13, 27)—a characteristically Old Testament image, which means, above all, Israel gathered together and returning home. One can therefore, in a certain sense, speak of the two peoples being 'complementary', and the fact that the Church at the present time is making giant efforts, using all its spiritual and intellectual powers, to win back the theology and spirituality of the Old Testament, demonstrates sufficiently that the idea is not an empty word. Individual conversions may be very fruitful; but the whole meaning and sense of the continued existence of Israel simply cannot be that Israel should be absorbed into the Church by multiplying them. Israel has a destiny as a people. And once Christians have opened their eyes to that fact they then will not merely think of the individual Jews in Israel, but think in terms of a better understanding and convergence between the two separated halves of the people of God. (5)

After what Démann has said, two questions become very clear: the problem of (prophetic) faith, and the problem of the (sacramental) land. In his endeavour to show that Pauline and Johannine Christianity are new departures, Buber placed the two forms of faith as far apart as possible. In doing so, however, he was able to save the 'faith' of Jesus and the Baptist by including it in the old prophetic faith of Israel, although some of the synoptic texts which appear to go back to the original words of Jesus give one pause, for there can be little doubt that Jesus, in his self-consciousness, went beyond the phase of the suffering servant of Isaiah. It is of no matter, for the moment, that in order to achieve and maintain his distinction between the two forms of faith, Buber invokes the time-honoured alliance between Jewish and liberal Protestant exegetes, and is condemned in consequence to accept their prejudices and the theological short-circuits that follow on them (for example, in the central question of the witnesses to the resurrection). (6) Nor are we primarily concerned with the artificiality of the antithesis between the two forms of faith (7): on the one hand a purely Jewish 'trusting faith', the faith of the human partner in the covenant who abandons himself to the prophetic leadership of the Lord of the Covenant, whose ways can never be known or fixed in dogmas, formulas and laws; the faith of the man who adapts himself to the task before him which is always a new task—and on the other hand an intellectual, hellenistic form of faith, an 'object faith' (I believe *that* Jesus is the Messiah) which is among Christians the sum total of faith, so that human confidence in God is ultimately measured by the 'object', as in the first Epistle of St John, where it occurs in an extreme form: 'Every spirit which confesseth that Jesus Christ is come in the flesh is of God: and every spirit that confesseth not that Jesus Christ is come in the flesh is not of God: and this is that spirit of anti-Christ, whereof ye have heard that it should come' (1 John 4, 2, 3).

The antithesis is artificial because the Old Testament faith is founded upon a similar objective and positive belief (a belief in a 'that' to use Buber's terms), that is to say upon the fact of the promise given to Abraham and all the consequences that flow from it, upon the authority of Moses and the sealing of the Covenant on Sinai, upon the promise of divine faithfulness which the prophets (from Nathan to David) all of them renewed. In that line of descent, Jesus is simply the last of the prophets. But while this is true it must also be said that this element of confidence, obedience and free adherence is no less spontaneous and fundamental in the New than in the Old Testament. It is much more important to stress that the Old Testament conception of faith, which Buber brings out so forcefully in opposition to the New Testament conception, really belongs to the *fons et origo* of Christian faith, and must be part of it, though no doubt it has not always been given the necessary prominence either in thought or in life, nor sufficiently stressed in the Christian's reflection upon his faith.

Buber begins by analysing Mark 9, 14-29. He makes it seem probable that when Jesus answered the despairing father's words, 'if thou canst do anything, have compassion on us and help us', by replying, 'if thou canst believe, all things are possible to him that believeth', he was referring in the first instance to himself. (8) This is echoed in the words of the Epistle to the Hebrews that Jesus is 'the author and finisher of our faith' (12, 2) which, following on Chapter 11, with its long list of Old Testament believers, makes the statement particularly forceful. Faith, there, means an absolute perseverance in the will of God through suffering and darkness and humiliation, the very same faith which the author had described previously, in Chapter 2, as Jesus's obedience, suffering and temptation in common with all his brethren (2,

9-18). That is the basic attitude of the saviour which makes him into the 'finisher' of the Old Testament notion of faith, and makes him into the author of the 'following' which is to come—and as for the author of the Epistle, where the notion of faith is concerned, it hardly matters to him whether a man lived and believed before or after Christ, for the ancients believed in expectation of him, believed towards him (he says of Moses: that 'esteeming the reproach of Christ greater riches than the treasures of Egypt' (11, 26), in the same way that the new believers believe after Christ and from him.

If, in the course of oecumenical discussions in recent years, Catholics have come to put greater emphasis once again on the factor which Luther underlined so vigorously and one-sidedly, and to stress the element of confidence and of a child-like obedience in faith side by side with the other element of 'believing because a thing is true', then it would simply be carrying on in the same direction and going a little further in conversation with the Jews to observe that the inmost core of Jesus's attitude to the Father was none other, ultimately, than that intended by the Old Testament in spite of the fact of its rising far above the level of the prophets and the holy men. If we regard a patient, obedient abandonment to the spirit of the Father leading on into difficulties and suffering as the basic act of our faith, then our conception of the following of Christ would be more inwardly one with our notion of our faith in him. When we imitate him and follow him on the path of obedience to the Father, we enter faith in its first and deepest form, the faith of the Covenant, which the servant of Jahweh fulfils in the name of the whole people through his vicarious suffering; thus Jesus becomes the high point of the bond between God and Man. Then the object of Old Testament faith (the 'that') coincides with the object of New

Testament faith as promise with fulfilment. What was said earlier about the Christological structure of Israel can now be seen to receive its full significance, and the same is true of Démann's view of the 'complementary' character of Judaism and Christianity.

The faith which we find in Mark 9, the faith that can do all things is described to us in the parallel passages in Matthew 17, 19, as something which the disciples of Jesus can truly imitate, and is held up to special praise in the Epistle of St James: the faith of the soul which puts undivided confidence in God and builds upon him (James 1, 6-8; 4, 8); the faith that can do all things, just as Elijah could do all things (5, 16-18) because faith and deed, faith and obedience to life are one. And if St Paul means precisely the same faith, which there justifies the sinner in Christ (and not a faith artificially emptied of its essential act, for after all St Paul thinks as a Jew), it is surely desirable that the Epistle of St James—too often overshadowed by the power and brilliance of St Paul—should in practice be given a larger place in Catholic thought, as is being done among Protestants. To St James, the union of faith and existence is freedom: man then no longer stands under the law, but in it, and so in the law of freedom (1, 25; 2, 21). That unity had already been achieved by Abraham when he answered the promise of God's word with the confidence of his deed, demonstrated on Mount Moriah (Jas. 2, 21), 'and he believed in the Lord and he counted it to him for righteousness' (Gen. 15, 6). (9) This may at first seem to stand in contradiction with St Paul since his conception of Christian freedom appears rather to consist in overcoming the Old Law than in fulfilling it (Rom. 6, 16ff; 7, 1ff). Yet he regards the whole law ('the royal law' as St James says, 2, 8) as culminating in Christ's command to love, and regards that command as coinciding with Christian freedom (Gal. 5, 13-14). And since St Paul takes the law as beginning with Moses, it abuts on either side on a living faith which precedes it *qua* foundation and follows it *qua* end and aim, so that the same direct line runs from Abraham to Christ, in both St Paul and St James.

Now in this perspective the prophetic dynamism of the Old Testament faith, as interpreted by Martin Buber, does not have to stand aside or distinguish itself from the New Testament faith as seen in the 11th chapter of the Epistle to the Hebrews, for example, where faith is abandonment to God in expectation of the fulfilment of Christ. Nor is there any need to differentiate the structure of the New Testament following of Christ from the Old Testament following of God, particularly since, according to Buber, the prophets teach that in Judaism it must always verify its position with reference to the social element. Fundamentally the only real change lies in the fact that the prophetic dynamism of the Old Testament is given a lasting basis and receives an outlet in the inner mystery of the divine as revealed: the doctrine of the Trinity is latent and presupposed in all that is most unique in Judaism.

But it is precisely that dynamic conception which makes the Zionist notion of the sacramental principle of Israel so questionable from a theological point of view, and throws doubt upon the absolute correspondence between the people of Israel and the Land of Palestine. It is surely clear that it is no longer valid from a Christian point of view—and it does not require the Crusades as a counter-proof to confirm the fact: Jerusalem in the post-Christian era cannot be looked upon even as a secondary centre of genuine significance. Nor is it clear that it provides a theme of vital interest to the people of Israel themselves. The fact that the Temple was destroyed is relevant in so far as it is a genuine eschatological symbol, but once the centre, the sanctuary, has ceased to exist; the Land can no longer have any biblical significance. The old cult cannot be restored, and even from an Old Testament point of view it is superannuated; it no longer corresponds to the present phase of religious consciousness.

The theological correspondence between people and land belongs, from a Christian point of view, to the preliminary phase of the movement towards Christ, who is the enduring Temple, home and country of the faithful. Nevertheless, Buber is most certainly right when he emphasises the correspondence between Israel and the realities of this world, its feeling for marriage and the family, and the political and social realities. And if the existence of Israel in the world since Christ, and quite particularly in the world of today, has a meaning and consequently a purpose, a precise significance, we should not be far wrong in regarding the defence of the natural order, to which Israel seems called, as an essential element in its mission. Israel is the temporal image of the whole earthly and heavenly Kingdom of God, whose coming 'in mirrors and riddles' is the Church of Christ. The Church must fulfil both tasks simultaneously; it must embody the Word of God and the flesh of Jesus Christ more fully in the temporal order, and at the same time uproot and transplant the world as a whole into the Kingdom of Heaven and time into the dimension of eternity. One may, however, add that the second task acquired such a significance in Christianity— for it was after all the new element—that the first aspect of its mission has not infrequently been neglected and has sometimes been forgotten. It should also be added that when the young Church was uprooted and separated from Israel—and when the newly uprooted community encountered innumerable forms of spiritualism and 'ex-carnation' in the philosophies of the hellenistic world—the Church fixed its attention as a general rule on the beyond, and tended to conceive the period of probation in this world predominantly in individualistic terms, with the result that it gave barely a thought to the other aspect, the future of mankind, not to speak of feeling any special responsibility for it.

As a result, there is a great deal in modern times which might have been informed and nourished by the Christian spirit and which has been allowed to escape its influence. Israel, on the contrary, was deeply involved in the whole process and took the road that leads to Utopia. But that could only have led to significant action if the two tendencies in Israel, the prophetic and the sacramental tendencies, had not been neutralised by a corrosive dialectic with the result that one tendency is always destroying what the other is building up—so that finally the destructive, negative, revolutionary tendency common to both alone remained operative. The influence of Israel in the world, and its prophetic driving force, can only be significant if they do not rush headlong into an absolutist, Utopian void, and if it is given a Telos, a meaningful end which, from the inner necessity of the situation, can only be Jesus Christ, the God-man, the Messiah who fulfils the covenant between God and man and is therefore in harmony with the immanent tendency of Judaism.

But that would be to presuppose, on the Jewish side, a desire and capacity to relax instead of accentuating a tendency to cling to some alternative absolute, which in fact is always heightened wherever and whenever the only possible, Christian, solution is rejected. Jewish-Christian history is, at any rate from a Christian point of view, an indivisible unity. There is no greater unity in the world, according to God's plan, than that between the Old and the New Covenant, except the unity of Jesus Christ himself who embraces the unity of the two covenants in his own unity. Any form of separatism and any suspicion of isolationism is fatal: Christianity when separated from the Old Covenant is always in danger of degenerating into Gnosticism, Marcionism or some form of Hitlerism. The Old Covenant, divorced from the Church, equally becomes gnostic and is in danger of becoming demoniacal. Any attempt to make it chemically pure and disinfect it of its Christian orientation, to reduce it to a self-sufficient principle, is profoundly unjust to the whole past history of Judaism; and, as we have seen, to do so is to halt its historical movement and turn it back upon itself. It is not possible to step off the moving platform of history, quite particularly if one lives in an historical religion. History cannot be dissolved in or dissolved into the philosophy of religion. And Israel can only really become conscious of its role in the Kingdom of God to the extent to which it is prepared to moderate its absolutist attitude, and allows itself to be saved in Christ; then it can receive the mission towards which it has always been drawn, the role which it abandons when it denies the transcendent character of the resurrection and the ascension. Israel before Christ knew that transcendence and looked towards those realities; its prophets and the prayers of its faithful were filled with that spirit. But the Israel of today has lost its sense of transcendence and only thinks of the here and now; and that strong feeling for the earth with its eschatological agnosticism, its refusal to think of the 'hereafter' as well as the 'here', is quite unbiblical.

But whatever its earthly task may be, and it can only be a

relative and preliminary one, Israel's mission to suffer is certainly biblical. It is a hidden, vicarious task. The suffering servant is one of the arrows hidden in God's quiver. Were it drawn forth it could achieve great things, but God wishes it to remain hidden. With his profound knowledge of Israel's role, Buber has said so over and over again. Everything else that can be said about Israel's task, the demand that it should be recognised by the nations of the earth, as well as all the discussions which go on within the Jewish community about their own understanding of their mission in history (which Buber has chronicled in *God and Magog* in a form that disconcerts and amazes the non-Jew)—all these are things that vanish in silence before the mystery of suffering about which all that one can rightly say is that it exists. Of that Israel may be certain, as both Old and New Testament testify. For Israel not only continues to exist down the ages in spite of itself, it has a tremendous will to exist for the sake of that mystery, which no one knows but God.

CHAPTER SEVEN

Conclusion

NOT EVERYTHING that is said in the course of a discussion touches the person addressed, and not everything even in a genuine dialogue reaches its goal—whether its aim is to confirm something, to give a warning, or simply to attract the listener's attention. Often enough the speaker simply expresses his own mind in a way that only differs from a monologue through being intended for the listener. It may belong to the core of the dialogue, but lead away from the centre, out to the circumference, as happens when the material produced ceases to be exchangeable or to provide a means of inter-communication. What the Christian has to say to the Jew in the last resort, the most precious thing he can offer, and the heart of the matter where he is concerned, may well seem so strange to the Jew that he pays no heed to it, thinking it cannot possibly be of any interest or use.

And yet these final words, these ultimate things, are spoken in such a way, since they come from the common heritage of revelation, that they may appear as the necessary fulfilment to the Jew, and as precisely what he should expect. Although both speakers in the dialogue relapse into silence as though falling back into their own isolation, and though each one of them can perhaps only point, in the final resort, to their own commission as he believes he has received it from God, yet the Christian's commission involves the fulfilment of the

Old Testament, and if only for that reason he cannot attain to a full consciousness of himself and his mission without at the same time acknowledging his relation to the Jew. As men they are of course distinct, possibly foreign to one another, and not necessarily with any sense of sympathy. But the limitations imposed by the tasks take no account of these all too human things. And so the final words must now be said, regardless of how they will be listened to.

The first thing to be said is this: Judaism, with its arms outstretched, reaches towards the messianic future of the world to embrace the absolute: the mystery of history in God. At one time Buber conceived of Judaism as the exponent of the East in Europe, outstripping and surpassing the monistic systems of Asia and, starting from a profound dualism, striving for the highest unity, so as to present it in a more effective and active form than Asia itself. And because unity is its aim, the cry of the absolute, with its dialogical character, is transposed into the innermost heart of being. 'It is not the word in itself that is the truth here, but life, life lived and the life to be lived; the word is only true by virtue of life.' (1) 'Doctrine may assign the Divine to the sphere of the beyond ... but the springs of life lead us on beyond that separation because they allow unity to come to birth in the free act of the complete man.' (2) But that unity, which is at once being and eternal, and is born of the encounter, is surely the absolute God? And then Buber came face to face with the Word in the Scriptures. His whole being was moved, and he learnt to bow before it as before the Lord and creator of all things, the giver of grace who needs nothing. And the fact that God speaks in that way and takes the form of the word for us, is in itself grace, the free movement of that wordless mystery. Buber's monistic metaphysic pales before a new and basic experience, and in order to describe it Buber mints two new terms with the definition which is normally reserved for the formulation of principles, and embodying a significant sequence: *Urdistanz und Beziehung* (1951) (3), distance and relationship. These terms certainly envisage, in the first place, man's fundamental capacity when faced by beings, things no less than men, for extracting or failing to extract a secondary *relationship* to them based upon a primary original *distance*, which is in fact the condition of a genuine encounter. But the experience which makes that primary occurrence possible, the awareness of something 'other' and its acceptance, depends ultimately upon a biblical experience of God and the word of God which is the very antithesis of any form of monism. For the Jew, the point at which thought and life really begin is the 'distance' between God and man. From that point of view everything falls into perspective; ancient as well as modern thought can be seen and judged as a whole. (4) The distance and relationship between men can only be in a healthy state within a sphere where the word of God is listened to; and the fact that God has been obscured or lost in the present world enfeebles the dialogue between men and obscures the dialogical principle itself. (5) Although Buber never falls into over-simplification and does not erect the 'I-Thou' relationship into a general, univocal principle which embraces the relation of man to man as well as of man to God, it is nevertheless a principle which Buber regards as decisively indicative of the relation of the creature to God. Mystical wisdom was the inspiration which led him as a young man to look for a union beyond words: the wisdom of 'distance' is the wisdom of the man full of years before the mystery of disparity. Both of them are ciphers with the help of which man can express the absolute. Buber allows them to co-exist side by side without attempting to resolve the question—'distance' is the primary phenomenon, the foundation upon which the subsequent relationship which follows is based: and that is nothing if not an open question. At this point the Christian can only offer an answer in silence and recognise the mystery: the absolute God himself is the identity of the three persons in one divine being, persons who proceeding one from another and being eternally other set forth the ultimate law of spirit, knowledge and love, but whose 'relationship' is not something subsequent or in any sense secondary, but is just as primary and essential as the unity of their being and personality. That mystery alone can hope to still the question of the significance of our creation and of the human spirit. And then the fact that the world exists—and not God alone—becomes clear and endurable. If that mystery is not visible in the background, then the dialogue moves relentlessly forward to Job's question to God; and it is difficult to see where and why the question should ever cease echoing in Judaic thought, eating down deeper and deeper with the passage of time, like a cancer.

And here we come to the second point: God's participation in his creation. In his first, monistic solution, Buber did not hesitate to make use of the idealistic, Asiatic language which is unavoidable here: the world is seen as the estrangement of God from himself, and God or consciousness returns to itself through the world. Buber is not propounding anything new at this point. The Jews had always overplayed 'the infinite distance' and grasped at the methods of gnosis; they discovered the myth of 'the glory of God, wandering, lost and living dispersed among things'; they listened to the sages of India or to the Greeks, and stumbled upon the idea of 'the salvation of God' or 'the idea of the reunion of the being of

God, which is separated from things, with the glory of God which has fallen upon the world' and so to the 'idea of the salvation of God through the creature: in that every soul reaches unity from duality, and every soul becomes one with itself, God becomes one in himself.' (6) The vista was then open on to Buddha, Laotse, Plotinus and Spinoza, and on to the speculations of the medieval Kabbala, and to the background which it shared with the Hassidim. Buber cannot simply discard all that myth, but neither can he take it over without judging it in the light of the Bible. In his early philosophy, divinity is found on both sides: in being and becoming or, since God is spirit, in eternal love and in the decision in time which touches the eternal. Here we have the root and justification of Jewish Theurgy, which is rejected *qua* magical power but accepted in the form of the 'absolute' act of the one who suffers, abandoning himself to God, as *Jichud*, but enveloped in a holy veil of mystery. Man is still, according to this doctrine, the helper of God. (7)

The alternatives are inescapable: either God is eternally sufficient unto himself, in which case the tragedy of his creation is a matter which does not concern him; or the tragedy is of great moment, and God is engaged on the side of the world, and its suffering is not a matter of indifference to him—something of him, his *Schechina*, suffers with it. And that surely corresponds to what the Christian calls 'uncreated grace', the communication of Holy Spirit? For we read that we can 'grieve' the Holy Spirit (Eph. 4, 30), 'quench' the Spirit (1 Thess. 5, 19) and that he longs and groans for the day of salvation: 'the Spirit itself maketh intercession for us with groanings which cannot be uttered' (Rom. 8, 26). Perhaps, then, we are bound by these mysterious words, prevented from adopting an all too critical attitude to the myth which Buber himself severely criticizes while making use of it. For we are tempted to say that it is at this point that Buber crosses the frontier of the Old Covenant in the one way possible to him and borrows something from the Cross of Christ. The greatest mystery of the Old Testament, the mystery of the suffering servant of God, implies the recognition of vicarious suffering, though there is nothing to suggest that his suffering is itself divine. But in order to bring out the mystery of the ultimate solidarity of God with his suffering creation, while avoiding interpreting that solidarity in an incarnational sense, there was only one thing to do, and that was to make use of kabbalistic pantheism, in spite of the fact that it appears to come into flat contradiction with the principle of 'distance'. What is the *Schechina*, where is the witness to it and the sanction for it? And if we remain obedient to the word of God, how can we cross the line of demarcation traced by the notion of the 'distance' between God and creature at any other point than the one shown to us by God himself in Christ, which is at the point of the hypostatic union? Are we not compelled to interpret the passages about the groaning spirit from this point of view, as indeed the whole context of Romans 8 proves? And yet we Christians, too, must concede that the fundamental Christological fact implies going a step beyond the 'distance' between God and man promulgated by the Old Testament. The fact that God in the person of Christ, in his human nature, desires to take upon himself the sufferings of the world, demonstrates that that suffering is not indifferent to him, and that he is concerned and touched by it in his divine nature. We cannot assert both things at the same time: that God is inwardly concerned with the tragedy of creation, and simultaneously that he is inwardly untouched by it. Unless, of course, we understand God's transcendence in so high a sense that it allows him to participate freely. 'One can, and indeed must say as much, without being accused of being a Hegelian,' Karl Rahner writes. 'For it is after all true, it is part of dogma, that the Logos himself became man, and therefore himself became something which (formaliter) he was not always, and that therefore what he became—precisely as itself and through itself—is the reality of God. And if that is the truth of faith . . . then ontology will have to take it into account and be enlightened by it and concede that while God remains unchangeable "in himself", he can become "in the other", and that *both* statements can be made really and truly of the same God.' (8)

Buber clings to this mystery in spite of the fact that it seems to us Christians as though he cannot possibly give it a biblical foundation except by taking into account the Christian fact of the incarnation. But that mystery also compels us Christians to interpret the Christian fact in a deeper and more daring way than we are accustomed or inclined to do. It is a good thing that this convergence of ideas should once again come into view, that we should both of us be brought up against the identical marvel that we cannot put into words, and that at the very limit of human power of expression we should both withdraw into silence and prayer. That will also ensure that whatever we expect the unveiling of the mystery to bring forth we both ultimately wait for the same thing. 'For there is only one theological hope.' (9)

Notes and References

Notes and References

The references are given as they appear in the German edition. This solution has been adopted because the works referred to are not by any means all of them translated into English, while some of them occur in different versions in England and America. To complicate the position, many of the German editions quoted are unobtainable. Unsatisfactory as the solution is, it seemed the only possible one.

For the sake of those who wish to pursue a reference, I give below a list of the German titles and their English or American counterparts wherever I have been able to identify them.

1. *Kampf um Israel. Reden und Schriften* 121-132. Some of this work has appeared in *Mamre*, some of it in *Tales of the Hassidim* (see no. 22).

2. *Gog and Magog—For the sake of Heaven* (U.S.A., 1945).

3. *Zwei Glaubensweisen—Two Types of Faith*, Routledge, 1951.

4. *Die Schriften über das Dialogische Prinzip* comprises:
   a) *I and Thou.*
   b) *Between Man and Man.*
   c) A *Postscript* not translated.

5. *Reden über das Judentum*—no English equivalent.

6. *Königtum Gottes*—no English equivalent.

7. *Die Stunde und das Erkenntnis;* no English translation.

8. *An der Wende;* Possibly the title *At the turning* (1952) and listed in Dr. Friendmann's bibliography is a translation which has not appeared in England.

9. *Moses;* in English under the same title.

10. *Sehertum, Anfang und Ende;* not in English.

11. *Pfade in Utopia; Paths in Utopia*, Routledge, 1949.

12. *Israel und Palästina; Israel and Palestine,* East & West Library, London, 1952.

13. *Die Jüdische Bewegung;* no English.

14. *Die Chassidische Botschaft;* no English.

15. *Ich und Du; I and Thou.*

16. *Urdistanz und Beziehung;* 'Distance and Relation', *Hibbert Journal* and *Psychiatry,* U.S.A., 2 May 1957.

17. *Gottesfinsternis; Eclipse of God,* Victor Gollancz, 1953.

18. *Bilder von Gut und Böse,* Hegner, Cologne, 1952; *Images of Good and Evil.*

19. *Right and Wrong* translated from the German Ms. *i.e.* no German.

20. *Jewish Mysticism*—German not given.

21. *Die Erzählung der Chassidim* exists in two versions: *Tales of the Hassidim,* New York, Schocken Books, 1947 (London, Thames & Hudson), and *Tales of the Hassidim, The later Masters,* do. 1948 . . . 1955, though as the German volume is a collection of articles, like so much of Buber's published work, it is difficult to identify.

22. *Between Man & Man* is partly from the Hebrew as are both *The Prophetic Faith* and *Der Prophetische Glaube.*

23. There appears to be no German original for *Pointing the Way,* though it may be taken from *Hinweise,* Zürich, 1953.

This list does not claim to be complete. I have simply followed other bibliographies in so far as they seemed to be useful to anyone anxious to follow up a reference in Dr Balthasar's notes—though all the quotations are translated from his text.

Chapter One.

1. 'Kampf um Israel' in *Reden und Schriften* 1921-1932, p. 274.
2. *Ibid,* 299. 3. Gog und Magog (1940) 407. 4. H. Bietenhard: *Kirche und Synagogue in den ersten Jahrhunderten.* Bern. Theolog. Zft. 4. (1948) 174-192. 5. Gösta Lindeskog: *Die Jesusfrage im neuzeit-*

lichen Judentum, Uppsala 1938. 6. Rudolf Bultmann, Albert Schweitzer, Rudolf Otto, Leonhard Ragaz (*Zwei Glaubensweisen* 1950, 12-14). The Postscript to the last edition of the works on the Dialogical Principle published in Heidelberg, 1954, throws further light on the point. 7. The principal work is a monograph by Hans Kohn: *Martin Buber, sein Werk und seine Zeit, ein Versuch über Religion und Politik* (Hegner, Hellerau, 1930) which contains a very full chronological table and bibliography. There is also Maurice S. Friedmann's *Martin Buber, The Life of Dialogue* (University of Chicago Press, 1955, 2nd ed. 1956). There are some errors and omissions in the bibliography. 8. *Cf.* in the first place, Dr. Gertrud Luckner's 'Rundbrief zur Förderung der Freundschaft zwischen dem Alten und dem Neuen Gottesvolk—im Geiste der beiden Testamente'; Werthmannplatz 4, Freiburg im Breisgau. No. 10 (1951) contains a full review of *Zwei Glaubensweisen* by Karl Thieme and in Nos. 12/15 the same author examines Buber's and Scholem's studies of Jewish Gnosticism and Hassidism. As Buber is still little known in France it was not to be expected that the very informative *Cahiers Sioniens* edited by Paul Démann, NDS (68 rue Notre-Dame des Champs, Paris VIe), should concern themselves with Buber's work. Many views of the discussion between the two peoples occur in the two above-named journals, as in 'Judaica' and the new American periodical, 'The Bridge', which it is unfortunately impossible to discuss here. *Cf.* too Prof. Karl Thieme: *Martin Buber als Interpret der Bibel* Ztf. für Religions und Geistesgeschichte VI, i (1954) 64ff. Eugen Kogon and Karl Thieme: *Das Portrait: Martin Buber* in Frankfurter Hefte VI, 3 (March 1951), 195-200. Erich Przywara, *Judentum und Christentum* in 'Ringen der Gegenwart' (1929, II, 624-661); and the same authors *Humanismus* (1952) 724ff.

Chapter Two.
1. Augustine, *Contra Adversarium legis et Prophetarum*, I 2 C 5, PL 42, 649. 2. Augustine, *Sermo* 201, PL 38, 1032. 3. Augustine, *Tractatus adversus Judaeos* C 8, PL 42, 37, 1948. 4. Augustine, *Enarrationes in*

Psalmos, 148, N 17; PL 37, 1948. 5. *Die Erneuerung des Judentums* (in *Reden über das Judentum*, Gesamtausgabe 1923, 54). 6. *Ibid*, 51-52. 7. *Ibid*. 87-88. 8. *An der Wende. Reden über das Judentum* 1952, 24-31. 9. *Königtum Gottes* 1936, 3-12. 10. *Der Jude in der Welt* in *Die Stunde und die Erkenntnis* 1936, 42. 11, *Ibid*. 44. 12. *Cf.* Strack-Billerbeck II, 525-526. 13. *Christus, Chassidismus, Gnosis*. A reply to Rudolf Pannwitz in *Merkur* VIII (Oct. 1954) 923-929. The sharp tone of the reply is not difficult to understand. Pannwitz (in his article on Hassidism in the September number p. 810-822), in spite of an evident effort to interpret Buber correctly, protested against the way in which he 'derived' Christianity from Judaism ('Christ . . . is a new beginning, a wheel that moves of itself. One cannot derive him from something else, construct him from other elements nor take him to pieces'); and on the other hand described the God of Israel as an earthbound tribal God, and 'that implies a terrible degree of narrowness and of being confined in an unchanging historical situation'. 14. *Kirche, Staat, Volk, Judentum:* in *Die Stunde und die Erkenntnis* 152.

Chapter Three.

1. Hans Kohn, *op. cit.* 16-17. 2. Above all see: *Mein Weg zum Chassidismus. Erinnerungen*. Frankfurt 1918. 3. *Cf.* Postscript to *Die Schriften über das Dialogische Prinzip*, Lambert Schneider, Heidelberg, 1954, where Buber defines his position vis-à-vis the personalist thinkers. 4. *Reden über das Judentum*, Gesamtausgabe, Frankfurt 1923. ix. 5. *An der Wende*, 3. Rede, 65. 6. *Die Erneuerung des Judentums* in *Reden über das Judentum* 51. 7. *Jüdische Religiosität*, *ibid*. 121. 8. *Der Glaube des Judentums* in *Kampf um Israel*, 1933, 31. 9. *Die Erneuerung des Judentums* in *Reden über das Judentum* 56. 10. *Der Mythos des Juden, ibid*. 140. *Moses* 1952, 19ff. 11. *Cf. Cheruth, ibid*. 227, where Buber asks that 'men should unite themselves to the deepest forces, the living, religious forces which . . . are revealed in teaching and law, but were not adequately expressed in teaching and law. They surrounded both in a formless cloud, and radiated through both in the dreams of the popular soul. . . .'

12. 'The centre point of Jewish religiosity, in the earliest times, did not reside in faith but in act.' *Die Erneuerung des Judentums, ibid,* 50. 13. *Sehertum, Anfang und Ende.* (1955) 23, 44ff. 14. *Moses,* 75-76. 15. *Königtum Gottes* 1936, 139. 16. *Ibid.* 171. 17. *Ibid.* 173. 18. *Der Geist des Orients und das Judentum* in *Reden* 69-99. 19. *Unser Bildungs-ideal* in *Dis Stunde und die Erkenntnis,* 93. 20. *Pfade in Utopia* 1950, 89. 21. Königtum Gottes, 143. 22. Thomas Aquinas, *Summa Theol.* 3 Pars q. 61 a 1.

Chapter Four
1. *Israel und Palästina,* 1950, 100-115. 2. *Reden über das Judentum* 90-91. 3. *Die Jüdische Bewegung,* 1916. 76. 4. *Ibid.* 84-85. 5. *Ibid,* 87. 6. *Reden über das Judentum,* 173. 7. *Ibid.* 42. 8. *Pfade in Utopia* 221-223. 9. *Die Chassidische Botschaft.* 1952. 17. 10. *Ibid.* 33. 11. *Ibid.* 57. 12. *Ibid.* 87-88. 13. *Ibid.* 133. 14. *Ibid.* 135. 15. *Ibid,* 138. 16. *Ibid* 143. 17. *Reden* 149. 18. *Die Stunde und die Erkenntnis,* 160. 19. *Die Chassidische Botschaft* 108-109. 20. *Gog und Magog.* 146. 21. *Israel und Palästina.* 58. 22. *An der Wende* (1952), 99. 23. *Cf.* Buber's important discussion of the whole problem in the Postscript to *Schriften über das Dialogische Prinzip.* Heidelberg, 1954, 287-305. 24. *Ich und Du* (Zürich 1947) 64. 25. *Israel und Palästina,* 107. 26. *Summa Theologica,* 1a 2 ae q 5 a 5ad 2. 27. *Reden,* 58-59. 28. *Die Chassidische Botschaft,* 109. 29. *Pfade in Utopia* 20-21. 30. *Ibid.* 153. 31. *Ibid.* 159.

Chapter Five
1. *An der Wende,* 14-15. 2. *Die Jüdische Bewegung,* vol. 1 (1916) 213. 3. *Reden,* 107-108. 4. *Ibid.* 83, *Jüdische Bewegung* I, 145, 209ff. 5. *Jüdische Bewegung* I, 74. 6. *Reden,* 177. 7. *Reden,* 133. 8. *Ibid,* 129. 9. *An der Wende,* 40. 10. *Israel und Palästina,* 9. 11. *Die Stunde und Die Erkenntnis,* 156. 12. *Israel und Palästina,* II. 13. *Kampf um Israel, Reden und Schriften* (1932) 396-397. 14. *Sehertum, Anfang, und Ende* (1953) 23. 15. *Die Stunde und die Erkenntnis,* 148. 16. *Ibid.* 148-149. 17. Karl Barth: *Kirchliche Dogmatik* II, 2 (1942). 18. Erich

Przywara; *Alter und neuer Bund* (Herold, Vienna, 1956). 19. Paul
Démann: 'Israel et l'Unité de l'Église, in *Cahiers Sioniens* no. I,
(1953), 1-24; Israël et Église, Essais de dialectique' (*Ibid.*
no. 9. 1950, 1-16). 20. Louis Bouyer: *La Bible et l'Évangile*
(in the series *Lectio Divina*, Editions du Cerf, Paris (1951).
21. *Tobias*, 13, 1-7. 22. *Jüdische Bewegung* (1916, 1921). *Kampf um
Israel* (1933). 23. Paul Démann: 'Le rassemblement des dispersés
d'après la Bible' in *Cahiers Sinoniens* IV, no. 10 (1950) 92-110.
24. *Kampf um Israel*, 397ff. 25. *Brief an Diognet*, cap v. 26. *Didache*,
Cap 9. 27. *Christentum als Neuheitserlebnis* (Herder 1939). 28. *Reden*,
168.

Chapter Six

1. *Der Restgedanke im Alten und Neuen Testament*, second excursus
in Johannes Munck: *Christus und Israel* (Aarhus University Press,
1956). 2. See Gottlob Schrenk: *Die Weissagung über Israel im N.T.*
(Zürich 1951). 3. Buber: *Sehertum, Anfang und Ende*, 24ff. 4. *An der
Wende, Reden über das Judentum*, 88-89. 5. 'Israël et l'Unité de
l'Église' in *Cahiers Sinoniens*, VII, 1953, no. I, 1-24. 6. In particular,
see Gösta Lindeskog: *Die Jesusfrage im neuzeitlichen Judentum. Ein
Beitrag zur Geschichte der Leben-Jesu-Forschung* (in *Arbeiten und
Mitteilungen aus dem ntl. Seminar zu Uppsala* edited by Fridrichsen,
VIII, 1938) which contains a very full bibliography. 7. *Zwei
Glaubensweisen*, 1950. 8. As in Lohmeyer: *Das Evangelium des Markus*
1954, 188, and Klostermann: *Das Markusevangelium*, 1936, 91
('although one really expects the worker of miracles [Jesus] to be
able to do everything, because he has the necessary faith,' 11, 23).
9. *Die fünf Bücher der Weisung*, revised edition 1954, 41. *Sehertum,
Anfang und Ende*, 28ff.

Chapter Seven

1. *Cheruth: Reden*, Gesamt Ausgabe, 218. 2. *Ibid*, 228. 3. *Urdistanz
und Beziehung*, 1951. 4. *Gottesfinsternis* 153. *Cf.* in particular to
Heidegger: 88ff. 115, and Buber's authoritative treatment of

Jung's facile arguments. 94ff: 'We really must get away from all this brilliant ambiguity!' (160). 5. *Ibid.* 145. 6. *Das Judentum und die Menscheit,* in *Reden,* 26ff. 7. *Die Chassidische Botschaft,* 102. 8. 'Probleme der Christologie von heute' in *Schriften zur Theologie* (1954) I, 202. 9. Paul Démann, *Cahiers Sioniens,* no. 10 (1950) 110.